How KAJUKENDO Became An American Martial Art

~The Unknown Story~

Mitch Powell

Self-published through Kindle Direct Publishing

This publication is designed to provide accurate historical accounts and information, but its accuracy is limited based on the memories and accounts of others.

ISBN: 979-8-9927608-0-4

Distribution and Sales

Amazon

DEDICATION

This book is dedicated to my wife Angel for her unwavering love and support. To my sons Matthew and Dean for becoming part of my Kajukenbo journey, and to Frank Lucero for taking me to train with Tony Ramos in 1975 and introducing me to Kajukenbo.

ACKNOWLEDGEMENTS

I would like to pay respect to my Kajukenbo teachers, Tony Ramos, Calvin Shin, Emil Bautista, and Joseph Davis. To John Bishop for all the work that he has done in researching and sharing the history of Kajukenbo. To Jim "Kimo" Emperado Smith and Dr. Glen Fraticelli for honoring me with the title of historian for the Kajukenbo Self-Defense Institute and for sharing their time and Kajukenbo resources. To Albert Saddler for providing so many prized Kajukenbo historical documents and photographs and to Loran Kelley for his editing assistance and creative input. Without all of them, this book would not be possible.

FOREWORD

By Dr. Glen Fraticelli

From the tender age of six, my life has been intertwined with the discipline of martial arts. My earliest lessons were in boxing, imparted by my father, who honed his skills on the rugged streets of Kalihi, Hawaii—the very birthplace of Kajukenbo. This unique martial art, conceived in the late 1940s, seamlessly blends elements of karate, judo, jujitsu, kenpo, and boxing, embodying a practical approach to self-defense.

In 1971, a pivotal moment reshaped my path: I watched Bruce Lee's "The Big Boss." The film ignited a fervent passion within me, compelling me to explore martial arts beyond the boxing ring. During family visits to my Uncle Joe's home in Pacifica, California, I often noticed cloth silhouettes of karate figures adorning his garage window. Unbeknownst to me then, Uncle "Joe" was none other than Joe Halbuna, a Pioneer in Kajukenbo.

Eager to delve into this new world, I expressed my desire to transition from boxing to martial arts. My father, initially hesitant, eventually agreed—on the condition that I arrange my own transportation. Undeterred, I discovered a local dojo and, for the next two years, embarked on a daily 15-mile bicycle journey each way to train.

By 1976, my dedication led me to an elite, handpicked fighting team. My boxing background instilled a preference for full-contact encounters, which often resulted in disqualifications during point-based competitions due to excessive force. Our coach, soon departing for China to pursue opportunities in martial arts cinema, introduced us to a Kajukenbo instructor.

Despite my familial connection, Kajukenbo was a revelation to me. Its emphasis on robust, street-effective techniques resonated deeply, and I embraced it wholeheartedly. However, our training was predominantly combat-focused. While we mastered the tactical applications and adopted a street-smart mindset, the rich history and formal katas of Kajukenbo were not taught.

In 1985, my journey through the world of Kajukenbo led me to a pivotal encounter with Ahgung Tony Ramos, a distinguished Pioneer of Kajukenbo. While I was familiar with the commonly told history of the "five masters" who founded Kajukenbo and the five Pioneers who introduced it to the mainland United States, I had never delved deeply into its origins until meeting Ahgung.

I became part of Ahgung's household, living with him and his family for nearly two years. During this period, we spent countless hours "talking story," as he shared the rich, intricate, and raw history of Kajukenbo. Through his vivid narratives, I was transported back to the very streets of Kalihi, Hawaii, where my father had grown up. The names and events Ahgung recounted were the same ones my father had spoken of, painting a tapestry of shared experiences and heritage. Remarkably, my father once lived on Auld Lane, the same street where Kajukenbo's founder, Sijo Adriano Emperado, was raised. This revelation intertwined my personal history with the foundational roots of Kajukenbo, deepening my connection to this martial art. I developed an insatiable desire to learn more about Kajukenbo's past, eager to preserve and honor the legacy was my calling.

Fast-forward to 2012, after dedicating 37 years to Kajukenbo and being appointed Deputy Chief of the Kajukenbo Self-Defense Institute (KSDI) by Senior Grandmaster Dechi Emperado, I had the privilege of engaging in a profound discussion about Kajukenbo's history with Grandmaster Mitch Powell. This conversation ignited a shared passion for uncovering the roots and evolution of Kajukenbo, leading us to embark on a decade-long journey of research and discovery. Our commitment to Kajukenbo's legacy led us to meticulously examine historical records, news articles, personal accounts, and archival materials. Throughout this decade-long endeavor, our combined expertise facilitated a comprehensive exploration of Kajukenbo's origin. This collaboration stands as a testament to the power of shared passion and the relentless pursuit of true Kajukenbo history.

While we both engaged in extensive research and discovery, Mitch was all in. He meticulously organized the historical details, crafting documented summaries of the lives and experiences of Kajukenbo's founders and key figures. His ability to bring order to the vast history of our art was unmatched, ensuring that the legacy of Kajukenbo was preserved with accuracy and depth. His expertise in research and writing and dedication to authenticity ensured that every detail was verified and documented. I recall vividly a moment after reading one of Mitch's articles, I said to him, "Mitch, you should write a book." He simply replied, "I am." His work, this book, is an "honoring" of the Kajukenbo Founders, Pioneers, and all that followed. I am honored to write this forward and was privileged to be on part of this worthy journey.

This book is more than history; it is a living testament. A chronicle of warriors past and present, of those who have walked this path with sweat on their brows and "blood on the mat." It is a tribute to the pioneers, the masters, the seekers, and to all who stand today in the lineage of this art, breathing life into every strike, every stance, every step forward.

May these pages be both a mirror and a lantern—reflecting where we have been, illuminating where we have yet to go. For Kajukenbo is not just an art. It is a way. It is a promise. It is a legacy that endures.

Dr. Glen Fraticelli
Deputy Chief KSDI
Kajukenbo Grandmaster

In life we are only "given" one breath
Upon birth we inhale
Upon death we exhale
What happens in between is up to you

ABOUT THE AUTHOR

Mitch Powell lives in Las Vegas, Nevada with his wife Angel. They have been married since 1982 and have two sons Matthew and Dean, who are both Kajukenbo black belts. In June of 2024 they welcomed the birth of their first grandchild, Adalynn Grace Powell.

Mitch is a lifelong Kajukenbo practitioner who started his Kajukenbo training in 1975, at the age of 15, under Ahgung Tony Ramos. In the years that followed Mitch trained in Kajukenbo from Sr. Grandmaster Calvin Shin, Great Grandmaster Emil Bautista, and Great Grandmaster Joseph Davis. In 2009, Mitch was promoted to the rank of 9th degree, red/silver belt, with the title of Grandmaster.

Mitch is the historian for the Kajukenbo Self-Defense Institute and the Chairman of the United Kajukenbo Federation, an organization created to help preserve and promote the Emperado-Method of Kajukenbo.

Lastly, Mitch is a retired sergeant with the Oakland Police Department in Oakland, California and holds an associate's degree in psychology, a bachelor's degree in criminal justice management, and a master's degree in liberal studies/criminal justice.

PREFACE

The martial art of Kajukenbo was founded in 1947 but continues to grow even today with new branches, new methods, and new ideas. The purpose of this book is not to capture the entire history of Kajukenbo but instead focuses on how Kajukenbo became a martial art and the role played by those who founded and created Kajukenbo.

With that said, if you are new to Kajukenbo this book with provide you with a wealth of information, but I want to stress that I wrote it primarily for those who have a background in the art—the students, the teachers, and the masters. I want this book to be a part of the history they share with others.

Whenever possible the source of information for this book has been extracted directly from the numerous interviews featuring one or more of the Kajukenbo founders. In rare cases, information provided by the founders may contradict one another so all views are shared along with supporting documentation allowing readers an opportunity to develop their own opinions. I cannot guarantee complete accuracy of all the events and details in this book because the accuracy depends on the memories and accounts of others.

If you are familiar with the history of Kajukenbo, especially the claim about Kajukenbo being created by five martial arts masters, you are really going to want to read this book.

I am the historian for the Kajukenbo Self-Defense Institute, an organization established by Adriano Emperado, the founder and creator of Kajukenbo. In addition, I am a trained investigator with a background in research and more than fifty years of training in the martial art of Kajukenbo. Given all of that, historical accuracy is extremely important to me and is the basis for this book. This story you are about to read on how Kajukenbo became an American martial art has never been shared publicly.

INTRODUCTION

I did not plan to write a book about Kajukenbo. Not initially anyways. As far as I was concerned John Bishop had already written the Kajukenbo bible back in 2006 with his book *KAJUKENBO, The Original Mixed Martial Art.* Bishop put in the work. He did the research, conducted the interviews, located the historical photos, and wrote an amazing book.

Then in 2017, David Tavares added a missing piece of the Kajukenbo puzzle with his book, *Black Robe, The Kempo/Kajukenbo Connection* when Tavares identified the authentic martial arts training background for Kajukenbo founder George Chang. That was the first time Chang's real training history was shared publicly.

Throughout most of my life the story about the development of Kajukenbo was centered on the art being created by five martial arts master's with each one being a master of a different martial art. While reading and reviewing Bishop's book I remember being surprised by the history he shared because for the first time there was an historical account on Kajukenbo that didn't call the founders martial arts masters, and it also didn't say each one trained in just one martial art. Instead of those claims, Bishop provided the training history of the Kajukenbo founders, and he explained that four of the five had training in multiple disciplines.

Inspired by Bishop's book, and training in and teaching Kajukenbo for decades by that time, I knew I wanted to learn even more. I had a lot of questions running through my mind. If the Kajukenbo founders were masters, who promoted them? When? Who was Choo's Tang Soo Do master? Who was Holck's judo master? How long did Ordonez train in Seikeno Ryu jujitsu? Under what teacher? Was Chang really a kung fu master?

Considering there were so few black belts in Hawaii in the 1940s, I found it extremely difficult to believe a karate master, judo master, jujitsu master, kenpo master, and kung fu master all in their early twenties came together to combine their arts and create Kajukenbo. The odds against that are just ridiculously high.

At that point in my life, I was just a few years away from finishing a law enforcement career with the Oakland Police Department that began in the 1980s. I had completed thousands of investigations and would soon complete a bachelor's degree and then a master's degree in criminal justice-related fields, which required an extensive amount of research. As a trained investigator with a background in research and a desire to know more, I decided it was time to put my skills to use and do a deep dive into the early history of Kajukenbo.

I spent the next decade researching and writing stories based on the information I was learning, which I often shared with my Kajukenbo students, colleagues, family, and friends. In 2017, with the assistance of Dennis Peterson, Albert Saddler, Walt Schuld, and Sam Carter, we formed the United Kajukenbo Federation to help preserve and promoted the Emperado Method of Kajukenbo. After doing so, Loran Kelley helped us take things a step further by creating and supervising the ukfcertified.com website where we share some historical information about the early development of Kajukenbo as well as the techniques and forms used for the Emperado-Method.

From my research and writings, Chief Jim "Kimo" Emperado Smith and Deputy Chief Glen Fraticelli appointed me the official historian for the Kajukenbo Self-Defense Institute, an organization established by Kajukenbo founder and creator Adriano Emperado. The honor they bestowed up me is one I greatly appreciate as a Kajukenbo practitioner and researcher.

In the last couple of years, I found myself as a regular guest on the Social Gelo podcast with host Angelo Ferrer, discussing the history of Kajukenbo. In doing so, we have reached thousands of viewers. I say this proudly because I value every opportunity to share my research, so others may acquire a better understanding of the history of Kajukenbo.

All of this brings me to the reason I decided to write this book on how Kajukenbo became an American martial art. I have written historical articles for years, created a website to help educate others on the early history of Kajukenbo, and routinely share my research through podcasts but the false Kajukenbo narratives continue. Just like John Bishop, I have tried so hard over the years to dispel those false beliefs about Kajukenbo and its founders, but they have been told for so long and repeated so often it's like they have been etched in stone.

My hope is that this book will finally allow others to understand and share the real story about how Kajukenbo became a martial art and the role played by the art's founders and creators.

~Grandmaster Mitch Powell

TABLE OF CONTENTS

Chapter 1

THE "FIVE MASTERS" STORY

Nearly everything written about the early history of the martial art of Kajukenbo tells the most majestic and grandiose story about how this art was developed and the five men credited with creating it. In this story, Kajukenbo is said to have been created in 1947 by five martial arts masters. Each is described as a master of a different martial arts style. Adriano Emperado is a master of kenpo-karate. Joseph Holck is a master of judo. Frank Ordonez is a master of Seikeno Ryu jujitsu. Peter Choo is a master of Tang Soo Do karate, and Clarence Chang is a master of Sil Lum kung fu.

The story goes on to say that together these five martial arts masters went on to blend the very best movements and effective techniques of their individual arts of karate, judo, jujitsu, kenpo, and boxing (Both Western and Chinese styles) together into a single martial arts style which they named Kajukenbo. A name created by combining the letters KA for karate, JU for judo and jujitsu, KEN for kenpo, and BO boxing.

As a Kajukenbo practitioner for more than five decades I can tell you that was the history I read and understood most of my life. Kajukenbo was created in 1947 by five martial arts masters, and each was a master of a different martial arts style. That is what you would find in the stories written about Kajukenbo and that was what you were told by your teachers. Even now when asking the question in a popular AI search engine was Kajukenbo created by martial arts masters? The response I received was *"Yes, the creators of Kajukenbo were indeed martial arts masters!"*

If the "Five Masters" story can be found everywhere even in an AI search engine it must be true, right? As the official historian for the Kajukenbo Self-Defense Institute I am here to tell you the "Five Masters" story is not true. The founders were not even black belts when they first got together. In addition, Kajukenbo was not really created in 1947. Holck was not a master of judo. Ordonez was not a master of Seikeno Ryu jujitsu. Choo was not a master of Tang Soo Do karate, and Chang was certainly not a master of Sil Lum kung fu. Chang's first name was also not Clarence.

Through years of research, I discovered most of the history being offered about Kajukenbo has been greatly romanticized, often misquoted, and contains significant embellishments about the art, the founders, and the role each played in the martial art's development. In addition, that compromised history has been retold, copied and reprinted so many times over the years that it is now considered to be factual. It is my belief that the retelling and reprinting of the false narrative year after year is what continues to fuel the "Five Masters" story, especially on websites.

While it may appear that my writing is designed to discredit the history of Kajukenbo and its founders, I assure you it is not. In fact, the purpose of this book is to share the amazing story that is Kajukenbo. Not the one about the five fictitious martial arts masters, but the one about the five Hawaiian born men in their early twenties who were surrounded by poverty, death and war. The five men who somehow figured out how to combine their striking and grappling knowledge together secretly while still training with their teachers. The five men who somehow put into place the foundation of what would become a martial art that can now be found all around the world.

The real story about how Kajukenbo became an American martial art is so much more interesting and compelling than the phony "Five Masters" story because it was not started by five martial arts masters. Kajukenbo was started by a brown belt and four white belts. The odds of a brown belt and four white belts coming together to create a martial arts style recognized around the world is astonishing and if you are anything like me, this story will cause you to gain an even greater appreciation and respect for the founders and creators of Kajukenbo and the art they developed.

Chapter 2

RESEARCHING KAJUKENBO'S HISTORY

In trying to gain the best possible understanding of how Kajukenbo became a martial art and finding out the role each person played in the founding and creation of Kajukenbo my first step was to collect as much credible information as I could find about Kajukenbo and those associated with its development.

Fortunately, there are several recorded interviews featuring one or more of the Kajukenbo founders. Hearing the questions answered and the information provided directly by them is invaluable. The most significant of those recorded interviews that I reviewed are as follows:

- The 1987 Tucson "Founders" interview conducted by Vince Black featuring Adriano Emperado and Joseph Holck.
- The 1987 Panther Production interview conducted by Joseph Jennings featuring Adriano Emperado and Gary Forbach.

- The 1992 "Founders" interview conducted by Vince Black featuring Adriano Emperado, Joseph Holck, and Peter Choo.
- The 1992 "Emperado Speaks" interview conducted by John Bishop and featuring Adriano Emperado.

In addition to reviewing the recorded interviews, I gained further insight from books by John Bishop, Bruce Haines, and David Tavares as well as newspaper articles, military records, personal interviews that I conducted, and documents and photographs I received from colleagues. I listed some of my research information here for the readers because I refer to many aspects of it in the chapters explaining the history, especially the interviews featuring the Kajukenbo founders.

My Research Includes:

- Reviewing *Kajukenbo, The Original Mixed Martial Art* by John Bishop.
- Reviewing *Black Robe, The Kempo/Kajukenbo Connection* by David Tavares.
- Reviewing *Karate and its Development in Hawaii to 1959,* a thesis at the University of Hawaii by Bruce Haines
- Reviewing the Centuron Negro (Black Belt) interview conducted by John Bishop featuring Adriano Emperado.

- Reviewing newspaper articles from the 1940s and 1950s related to Kajukenbo and the founders.
- Reviewing magazine articles related to Kajukenbo and the founders.
- Reviewing personal letters received from Adriano Emperado.
- Reviewing obituaries of those related to Kajukenbo.
- Obtaining military records from the National Personnel Records Center.
- Obtaining photographs related to Kajukenbo and the founders.
- Obtaining excerpts from Emperado's unpublished book.
- Obtaining information from Jason Groff, the inheritor of the Ordonez Kajukenbo Ohana.
- Obtaining the 1957 school admission forms and school patches for the Wahiawa Kajukenbo school, as well as George Seronio's black belt book, and early Kajukenbo photos from Albert Saddler, the grandson of George "Pauly" Seronio.
- Obtaining photos of Joe Halbuna from his daughter Ilona Halbuna.
- Obtaining Photos of Charles Gaylord from his daughter Kelly Gaylord McCormick.

- Obtaining information and photos of Tony Ramos from his son-in-law David Amiccuci and daughter Leah Ramos Amicucci.
- Obtaining information through a personal interview of John Kanahailua, one of John Leoning's first students at the Kalihi Kajukenbo school and obtaining photos.
- Conducting a personal interview with Joseph Holck's son, Barry Holck.
- Conducting a personal interview with James Roberts, a Wahiawa school black belt who trained under Emperado.
- Conducting a personal interview with Carlos Bunda, one of John Leoning's first black belts.
- Conducting multiple interviews with John Ramos, the brother of Tony Ramos.

As you can see, I have gone to great lengths to find the evidence and documentation used in the writing of this book and to share that with the readers. It is my hope that by doing so and by systematically using this information to dispel the romantic and fabled "Five Masters" story, that the real history of the founding of Kajukenbo will now be told.

It's one thing to repeat what others say but it's something completely different when what you say is based on evidence and reason. Please know that I did my best to let both of those be my guide in dictating the outcome of this book. Now it is time to see how Kajukenbo became an American martial art.

Chapter 3

GROWING UP IN HAWAII

With the crash of the stock market in 1929 and the great depression that followed, Hawaii and the rest of the nation faced the worst economic crisis in modern history. The poverty and homeliness were devastating. In the early 1930s, Hawaii's unemployment rate went from three percent to as high as twenty-five percent and the number of visitors who made their way to the island for some fun in the sun declined by a record thirty-four percent in 1934. The economic times in Hawaii were dire.

For many of those who had wealth prior to the great depression they lost everything. For those who were poor prior to the great depression they just became poorer. It was during those challenging times that Adriano Emperado, Joseph Matsuno, Peter Choo, Frank Ordonez, and George Chang were born and raised.

While life was difficult for everyone, the Emperado family may have experienced even more of a struggle. By the mid-1930s, Emperado's parents divorced, and he ended up as a preteen moving to Kauai where he lived with his half-brother Hilario for a year or so before being able to return to the Kalihi area and his family. That meant Emperado suddenly had to live apart from his mother, father, brother and sisters as their family dynamic changed drastically. While challenging as that must have been for Emperado, he took something positive from the experience. That is when he learned the 12-strikes of the escrima system.

In 1938, Matsuno found an interest in jujitsu and joined a Danzan Ryu jujitsu class. He was 11 years old. About the same time Choo became interested in boxing, so he was signed up for lessons at the Joe Lynch gym. By 1940, Choo had his first ring fight. A year later, Chang began training in kung fu and Ordonez joined the same jujitsu class as Matsuno, leading to a lifelong friendship.

Just after 8 a.m. on December 7, 1941, their entire world changed when the Japanese military executed a sneak attack and bombed Pearl Harbor in Oahu, killing more than 2400 people and destroying over 300 planes and 20 U.S. ships. Emperado, Matsuno, Choo, Ordonez, and Chang were just elementary and first year high school students. Ordonez said he saw the attack from a window in his home. That attack led to America's full participation in World War II.

Unfortunately, for Matsuno the bombing at Pearl Harbor brought great anger and resentment towards anyone Japanese in Hawaii, so Matsuno's parents

Katsutaro and Mary Ann decided to petition the court to change their Japanese last name to protect the wellbeing of their five minor children.

On January 25, 1943, that petition was granted by Acting Governor of Hawaii, Ernest K. Kai, and the last name of the children was officially changed from Matsuno to Holck, Mary Ann's maiden name. From that day forward Joseph Matsuno became known as Joseph Holck. He was 15 years old.

By the mid-1940s, Emperado, Holck, Choo, Ordonez, and Chang all joined the United States Army with some participating in the war and others in the aftermath of the war that officially ended on September 2, 1945, with the Japanese surrender. Ordonez said he joined because of the attack on Pearl Harbor. It's likely the others did so as well.

From growing up during the great depression to experiencing the bombing of Pearl Harbor as teenagers and the battle of World War II as young men, Emperado, Holck, Choo, Ordonez, and Chang faced some unbelievable obstacles in their early lives, but despite it all went on to proudly serve their country and by chance came together as a group to establish the martial art of Kajukenbo.

Chapter 4

THE FOUNDING OF KAJUKENBO

(1947-1949)

Adriano Emperado

A significant number of people believe Kajukenbo was created in 1947, however, research shows that it is not accurate. The year 1947 wasn't the year Kajukenbo was created. It was the year Kajukenbo was founded, meaning when Adriano Emperado, Joseph Holck, Peter Choo, Frank Ordonez, and George Chang first began training together.

In the Centuron Negro interview conducted by John Bishop, Emperado said it took two years of training together before the founders completed the development of their techniques and then gave their art a name. In the Tucson interview Holck provided a similar remark saying the founders trained together for a year or more before naming their art. That moves the point where Kajukenbo had a name from 1947 to 1948 or even as late as 1949.

In the Panther interview, Emperado said the founders were brought together when Ordonez told him he had some friends who wanted Emperado to teach them kenpo. Bishop repeats that claim in his book. In the Tucson interview Holck and Emperado both agreed that Ordonez and Choo organized the meeting that brought all five founders together. So, the purpose of that first meeting was not to create the martial art of Kajukenbo, but for Emperado to show the others some kenpo.

Between 1947 and 1949, Emperado, Holck, Choo, Ordonez, and Chang trained together and created their own unique martial arts techniques by combining their collective knowledge of karate, judo, jujitsu, kenpo, and boxing (Western and Chinese styles). Based on those techniques the founders went on to create their own martial arts style which they named Kajukenbo, a name created by taking letters from the various arts used to create the Kajukenbo techniques. The founders used KA for karate, JU for judo and jujitsu, KEN for kenpo, and BO for boxing. Since Hawaii was a territory of the United States, not only did the founders create a new martial arts style but they also created an American martial art. According to Emperado the founders then established the Black Belt Society as their own organization before disbanding in 1949.

THE FOLLOWING INFORMATION IS ESSENTIAL TO UNDERSTANDING THE 1947-1949 FOUNDING PERIOD OF KAJUKENBO:

Who are the five founders of Kajukenbo?

The five founders of Kajukenbo are Adriano Emperado, Joseph Holck, Peter Choo, Frank Ordonez, and George Chang.

What year did the founders start training together?

The answer comes from the 1987 Tucson, Arizona interview where Emperado and Holck were brought together for the first time in nearly forty years. The two sat side-by-side as they were interviewed by Vince Black. When Black asked them what year they began training together Emperado said, "47? 48?" while Holck responded at the same time saying, "48? 49?" Then they looked at each other and at the same time said, "48?" while they both nodded their heads yes, but still weren't 100 percent sure. Holck then followed that by saying, "I think part of 1947 too." Emperado nodded his head yes once again in agreement. Based on what the two founders remembered and the way they answered the question it would appear the bulk of their training together occurred in 1948 and 1949, but they did start training together in 1947.

How did the founders get together as a group?

In that same interview Holck and Emperado agreed that Ordonez and Choo organized the training session that brought the five Kajukenbo founders together.

Where were the first training sessions?

In the Tucson interview Emperado said the five founders first trained together "A little bit" at Damon Tract, which was the location of Choo's family home. Emperado said after training a few times at Choo's home they decided to try each other out. At that point they made a date, and all five founders went to Kaheka gym where they tested their skills against each other (Kenpo against boxing, jujitsu against kung fu, etc.). From there they began training together at various locations including an abandoned military barracks located in Halawa Veteran's Housing across the road from where Ordonez lived.

Did the founders train secretly?

In the Tucson interview Vince Black asked Holck if his instructor Professor Okazaki knew that Holck was training with the group. Without hesitation, Holck and Emperado both responded immediately and simultaneously to Black saying, "No one knew!" Keep in mind when considering their simultaneous response that no one knew they were training together, Holck and Emperado had not seen each other for nearly forty years and both immediately provided that response.

What locations did the founders use for their training?

From the Tucson interview and a 1992 interview known as the "Founders" interview recorded in Hawaii featuring Holck, Emperado, and Choo with Vince Black as the interviewer, and from Bishop's book, we learn the founders trained at three primary locations: Kaheka Gym, located at 904 Kaheka Lane, Choo's family home, located at 574 P Road in the Damon Tract housing development, and at an abandoned military barracks across from Ordonez's residence at Halawa Veteran's Housing. In the Tucson interview Holck said the founders trained together at the abandoned military barracks for two years, making that their primary training location.

What led the founders to create techniques?

In the Founders interview, Choo explained that the idea of creating techniques of their own did not happen right away. That came about later when Choo was training in a Danzan Ryu jujitsu class at Kaheka gym taught by Sam Luke Sr. Choo said when he would use a boxing technique like a fake, he noticed the traditional martial artists were just lost. As Choo explained this with Emperado, Holck, and others looking on, Choo remained seated but held his hands in a boxing position and made bobbing and weaving head movements to demonstrate.

Choo said upon realizing this issue with traditional martial artists he suggested to Emperado that they take the best of each art and combine them so they could tackle every situation. Choo went on to say this was the beginning of the combination arts, meaning the point where they began combining their arts together.

How many techniques did the founders create?

From Bishop's book, we learn the group created grab defenses, punch defenses, and self-defense combinations against a knife and club but the exact number of techniques the founders created has never been revealed. In addition, it is probable that at least some of the techniques created by the founders may have been modified prior to Emperado establishing a formalized Kajukenbo curriculum in the 1950s while other techniques were most likely added.

Just before the Tucson interview, Vince Black and others participated in a seminar where Holck was present. During the interview Holck was asked by Black if any of the techniques that Black and the others were working on prior to the interview looked familiar? Holck responded, "They all looked familiar." Holck was very animated as he explained, "All the techniques you were working on—we used to do that!"

Did the founders create martial arts forms?

According to Emperado the forms found in Kajukenbo were not created by the founders during the 1947-1949 period. Emperado said he and his brother Joe created the Kajukenbo forms in the 1950s while teaching classes at the Palama Settlement.

What arts did the founders possess?

When taking this question into consideration it's important to keep in mind that the founders stopped training together and collaborating as a group in 1949. So, the training that I have identified and listed for each Kajukenbo founder only consists of their known martial arts and fight training history up to the year 1949.

Emperado, Holck, Choo, and Ordonez all continued to train in the martial arts after the group disbanded and each one went on to achieve a high martial arts rank and formal title. That training and rank information is not listed because it all occurred after the founders went their separate ways.

Adriano Directo Emperado

From Bishop's book, we learn Emperado was taught some boxing at a very young age by his father, and uncle. At age 11, he learned the basic 12 strikes of escrima from a person known to him as "Professor Alex." By age 13, Emperado briefly trained in jujitsu at the Young Buddhist Association under Professor Yamasaki and Professor Murata but became more interested in boxing and began competing in a local boxing league. At age 17, Emperado began training in judo at the Palama Settlement gym under Sensei Taneo. Emperado struck a deal with Taneo where Emperado taught boxing to Taneo and his son in exchange for judo lessons.

The National Personnel Records Center shows Emperado was drafted into the United States Army on December 22, 1945. He was 19 years of age. From those records and excerpts from Emperado's unpublished book, we know Emperado discharged from the army on March 17, 1947, and returned to Hawaii. It was at this time when Emperado's future brother-in-law Walter "Woody" Wood, Jr. told Emperado about kenpo and walked with Emperado down the street to Fred Lara's house where Emperado watched Lara practicing martial arts in his front yard.

Lara explained to Emperado that he was learning kenpo from William Chow and invited Emperado to come to the class where Chow taught, which was in the training hall on the second floor of the Columbus Welfare Building at 1183 Fort Street. Emperado went there and watched the class. Then Emperado met

Chow for the first time and became a kenpo student of Chow's. Emperado wrote in his memoirs all about this and said, "That was 1947."

Sometime within the seven months after Emperado began training from Chow he started training with Holck, Choo, Ordonez, and Chang. That timeline is based on records showing when Emperado most likely started with Chow which may have been March or April of 1947, and when Emperado reenlisted in the army and left Hawaii on October 31, 1947, enroute to Guadalcanal for what appears to be the remainder of the year. So, Emperado began training from Chow in maybe late March or early April and was gone by October 31st. That leaves about seven months of time for Emperado to learn kenpo from Chow and begin to teach kenpo to the other founders at their training sessions.

While Emperado trained with the other Kajukenbo founders from 1947 through 1949, he also continued to train from Chow and in 1949 was promoted by Chow to the rank of Shodan, black belt, 1st degree in kenpo jiu-jitsu. In his memoirs Emperado said he not only trained in group classes with Chow, but he would routinely pick Chow up from his home and they would train together for hours on most days.

Based on Emperado's known training history at the time the founders got together in 1947, boxing would have been Emperado's primary art, followed by about a year of judo, then maybe seven months of kenpo, some jujitsu, and knowledge of the 12 basic strikes of escrima. Emperado had no martial arts rank until he was promoted to black belt by Chow in 1949.

Joseph Matsuno Holck

In the Founders interview Holck explained that he did some boxing as a kid with his older brother (Wilbert "Sandy" Holck) growing up, but he wasn't that good, so he gravitated towards grappling. In 1938, Holck began training in Danzan Ryu jujitsu under Seishiro "Henry" Okazaki and continued that training until Holck enlisted in the United States Army.

The National Personnel Records Center shows Holck enlisted in the army on November 16, 1945, but other writings suggest Holck enlisted as early as 1944, when he was just 17 years of age. During basic training Holck's martial arts skills were recognized, leading Holck to become a hand-to-hand combat instructor. After WWII concluded, Holck was sent to Germany during the allied occupation where he served as a hand-to-hand combat instructor for the Army's 9th Infantry division.

In 1947, Holck returned to Hawaii and resumed training in Danzan Ryu jujitsu under Bing Fai Lau and Siegfried "Sig" Kufferath. It was at this time when Holck began training with Emperado, Choo, Ordonez, and Chang.

In an interview I conducted on March 3, 2021, with Holck's son Barry, I learned Holck was a brown belt when he began training with the other Kajukenbo founders in 1947 and he was the only member of the group with any martial arts rank. On July 14, 1948, Holck was promoted to the rank of Shodan, black belt, 1st degree, by Okazaki and Kufferath. It was after this promotion that Holck began training in Kodokan judo under Toshiaki Inouye. In 1949, Okazaki and Kufferath promoted Holck to Nidan, black belt, 2nd

degree, and awarded him his certificate of mastery (Kaidensho) and his instructor's scrolls (Mokuruku).

Based on Holck's known training history at the time the founders got together in 1947, Danzan Ryu jujitsu would have been Holck's primary art. Holck had a brown belt. In July of 1948, Holck earned a black belt and that is when Holck began training in Kodokan judo. In 1949, Holck earned a 2nd degree in Danzan Ryu jujitsu and received a certificate of mastery. Holck had no known rank in judo during the time he trained with the founders.

Peter Young Yil Choo

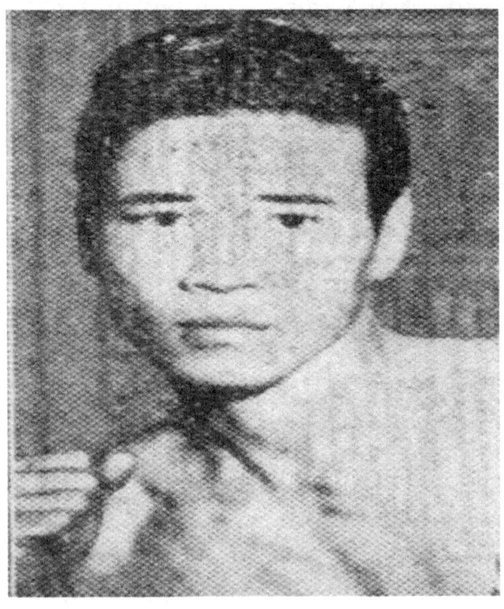

In an article dated August 12, 1953, from the Stars and Stripes military magazine titled, "*Choo's Daily*

Practice—Judo lifts veteran's ring hopes," Choo writes about his experience with boxing. Choo states he began boxing as a young boy growing up in Hawaii and by age 11, won the Joe Lynch boxing award. Choo's first amateur ring fight was in 1940.

In an article from the *Daily Kenirm*, a defunct Eastbay, California, newspaper dated May 30, 1959, titled, "*Hawaiian Uses Head on Bricks,*" Choo writes about his martial arts training. He states that he began judo training in Hawaii in 1943 and a couple of years later started training in karate under Professor James Mitose. Choo does not state the name of his judo teacher and research shows that Choo didn't train directly from Mitose, but from Mitose's student Thomas Young.

In an Ancestry newspaper article, Choo's first adult ring fight was on February 11, 1944, when he fought as a featherweight against Harry Pregana. Choo was a member of the Ledesma A.C. Boxing Club, and he was just 17 years old. From that point on, Choo was a frequent competitor on the Hawaiian amateur boxing circuit until 1952.

The National Personnel Records Center shows Choo enlisted in the United States Army on September 14, 1945, but other writings suggest Choo enlisted as early as 1944. By 1946, Choo was stationed at Ft. Shafter where he became a member of the army boxing team under the direction of coach Thomas Toyama. That is when Choo met fellow army boxing team member Frank Ordonez. According to the Ordonez Kajukenbo Ohana website after the two met, Choo began training with Ordonez in kenpo jiu-jitsu under Thomas Young, and in Danzan Ryu jujitsu with Ordonez and Joseph Holck under Sam Luke Sr.

In 1947, Choo began training with Holck, Emperado, Ordonez, and Chang. By that time Choo would have had approximately 80 rings fights based on the Stars and Stripes article which stated Choo completed a 12-year ring career in 1952 earning a record of 144 fights, 95 wins, 47 losses, 2 draws, and 45 knockouts.

Did Choo know Tang Soo Do?

In the Tucson interview, Holck made a comment that Choo knew some Tang Soo Do and contributed that to the early development of Kajukenbo. In addition, Emperado told Bishop, Choo said he learned karate from his father. Since Choo's father was Korean it was speculated that Choo learned Tang Soo Do.

Some key points that complicate Choo learning Tang Soo Do as a kid come from the fact that the art was not formally named in Korea until after Korea was liberated from Japanese rule in 1945. If Choo had been taught Tang Soo Do as a kid, the training would have predated the existence of Tang Soo Do by about a decade.

More importantly, Choo made no mention in the 1959 newspaper article about learning karate from his father or learning Tang Soo Do from anyone in his younger years. Choo said he learned karate from Mitose, which we know the teacher was Mitose's student Thomas Young. It's possible that Choo learned some karate as a kid from his father and failed to mention it, but nonetheless it would not have been Tang Soo Do.

Based on Choo's known training history at the time the founders got together in 1947, boxing would have been Choo's primary art, followed by some kenpo jiu jitsu and some Danzan Ryu jujitsu, and possibly some karate. Choo had no martial arts rank at that time or through the summer of 1948 as confirmed by photos.

I have included a photo taken by Ordonez of Choo in the summer of 1948 and a page of the letter written by Ordonez about the photos he took that day. The photo of Choo shows him in a white karate uniform wearing a white belt. Choo is preparing to break some boards with a punch. There are other photos in this series that provide a better view of the white belt, but this is the best image of Choo.

So even if Choo had some form of karate training at the time the founders got together it was not enough to earn any type of belt promotion.

Peter Choo Summer of 1948

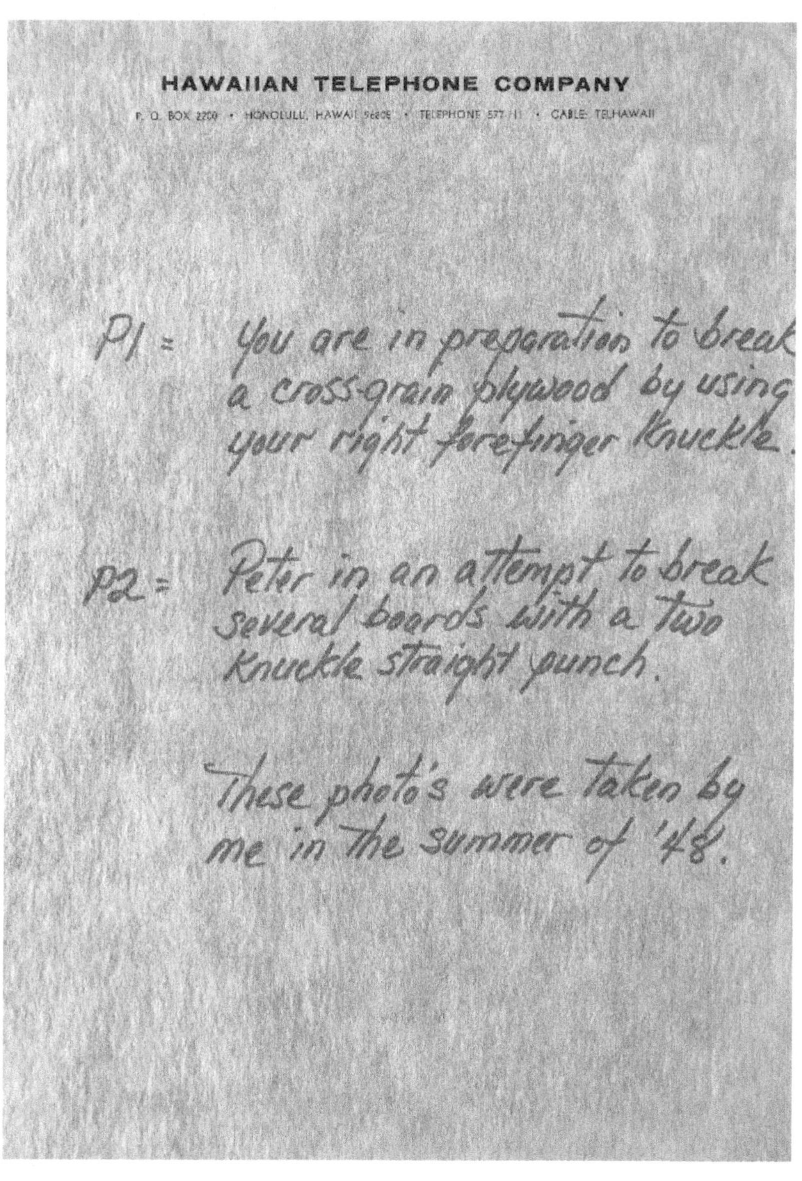

HAWAIIAN TELEPHONE COMPANY

P. O. BOX 2200 • HONOLULU, HAWAII 96805 • TELEPHONE 577-11 • CABLE: TELHAWAII

P1 = You are in preparation to break a cross-grain plywood by using your right forefinger knuckle.

P2 = Peter in an attempt to break several boards with a two knuckle straight punch.

These photo's were taken by me in the summer of '48.

Letter written by Ordonez about Choo's Photo

Frank Ferino Ordonez

From the Ordonez Kajukenbo Ohana website we read at the age of 14, Ordonez began training in Danzan Ryu jujitsu under Sam Luke Sr., who was teaching at Henry Okazaki's dojo. While training with Luke Sr., Ordonez met Joseph Holck.

The National Personnel Records Center shows Ordonez enlisted in the United States Army on May 21, 1946, while other writings suggest he enlisted as early as 1945. While stationed at Ft. Shafter in Hawaii, Ordonez joined the army boxing team under the direction of coach Thomas Toyama. That is when Ordonez met fellow army boxer Peter Choo.

Ordonez, Choo, and Holck then trained together in Danzan Ryu jujitsu from Sam Luke Sr., and Ordonez also cross-trained with Choo in kenpo jiu-jitsu from Thomas Young, the first student to earn a black belt from James Mitose.

In 1947, Ordonez began training with Emperado, Holck, Choo, and Chang. According to Jason Groff, the inheritor of the Ordonez Kajukenbo Ohana, Ordonez did not have any martial arts rank at that time.

It is often reported that Ordonez trained in Seikino Ryu jujitsu. According to Groff, that claim is not valid. Groff said Ordonez was asked about training in Seikeno Ryu jujitsu and Ordonez said he had no idea where that information came from, and it is not true. Research has failed to locate any martial arts style known as Seikeno Ryu jujitsu.

Based on Ordonez's known training history at the time the founders got together in 1947, boxing would have probably been Ordonez's primary art, but he also cross-trained in kenpo jiu-jitsu and Danzan Ryu jujitsu.

George Chuen Yoke Chang

Most martial arts accounts of George Chang record his first name as "Clarence" and report that at the age of 12, Chang traveled to Kwangtung, China with his father where Chang studied Sil Lum kung fu.

In the book, *Black Robe, The Kempo/Kajukenbo Connection*, author David Tavares was able to obtain a correct account of Chang's martial arts training. According to Chang's sister, who was Chang's last living relative, Chang never traveled back to China in his youth, and he did not train in Sil Lum kung fu.

Instead, Chang remained in Hawaii and at the age of 16 began training from famed kung fu instructor Wong Kook Fut, who taught a hybrid form of kung fu as well as the art of unicorn dance from his home in Kalihi. Chang was a student at Farrington high school at the time he began training under Wong Kook Fat and went on to earn a letter in basketball before graduating.

The National Personnel Records Center show Chang enlisted in the United States Army on February 26, 1946, following in the footsteps of his brother Charles, who was a sergeant in the 972nd stationed at Ft. Shafter. Chang became a crewman of a 40-mm gun in the 867th.

In 1947, Chang separated from military service, and in that same year began training with Emperado, Holck, Choo, and Ordonez.

Based on Chang's known training history at the time the founders got together in 1947, Chinese boxing or kung fu was Chang's only martial arts style. Chang had no known martial arts rank.

What arts could the founders have used to create their techniques?

Based on the known martial arts and fight training history from each founder's training background through 1949, they could have used the following arts to create their techniques for KA-JU-KEN-BO:

	Style	Contributor
KA	Karate	• Choo or "karate" came from kenpo-karate
JU	Judo Jujitsu	• Kodokan judo from Holck & Emperado • Danzan Ryu jujitsu from Holck, Choo, & Ordonez • Kenpo jiu-jitsu from Emperado, Choo, & Ordonez
KEN	Kenpo	• Kenpo jiu-jitsu from Emperado, Choo, & Ordonez
BO	Boxing	• Western boxing from Choo, Emperado, & Ordonez • Chinese boxing (kung fu) from Chang

How did Kajukenbo get its name?

In the Founders interview, Choo gave a detailed account on how Kajukenbo got its name and when that occurred. At the time of the interview Choo was seated between Holck and Emperado. Choo was very animated as he spoke, and he used his hands in a manner as if he was moving objects around a table. In his own words, Choo said, "We decided from letters on the coffee table." He then says, "Why don't we take K-A for karate, ah judo/jujitsu J-U, kenpo, KEN, and boxing, Chinese as well as American type boxing. Put together and let's see BO, KEN, JU, KA." At this point Holck, Choo, and Emperado all begin to laugh. Then Choo says, "JU, KEN, KA, BO," to which they all laugh some more. Choo then finishes by pointing with his finger forward as if he was pointing to the tabletop and adds, "I said, hey Joe, KA-JU-KEN-BO." Choo slaps his hands and says, "That was the first Kajukenbo. Damon Tract, 1947."

Although Holck and Emperado never challenged what Choo professed that day, in the Tucson interview which occurred five years earlier, Holck said he was the person who came up with the Kajukenbo name and in that interview Emperado agreed with Holck. In the Centuron Negro article written by Bishop, Emperado is quoted as saying, "Two years later when we finished, we needed a name to describe our combination system. Joe Holck came up with the name Kajukenbo."

If we believe Choo, then the Kajukenbo name was created as early as 1947, but that would have been nearly two years before the techniques were even created. Holck was adamant in the Tucson interview that he came up with the name a year or so after the group began training together. In fact, Holck said it several times in that interview as he was talking to Emperado, and Emperado agreed with Holck every time. Also, while being interviewed by Bishop, Emperado said Holck created the Kajukenbo name after the founders finished creating their techniques, which took two years.

If Emperado had claimed he came up with the Kajukenbo name that would have complicated matters a great deal, but he didn't. Emperado has repeatedly given credit to Holck for creating the Kajukenbo name. Since Emperado and Holck both agreed Holck came up with the name it seems reasonable to believe that Choo's claim of creating the name is just not accurate. Knowing the Kajukenbo name was most likely created in 1948 or even as late as 1949, eliminates the belief that Kajukenbo was created in 1947. As pointed out, 1947 was the founding of Kajukenbo, not the year it was created. Kajukenbo would not have existed without a name first.

Regardless of who created the name KA-JU-KEN-BO there is enough evidence to conclude the name was created during the 1947-1949 founding period, so we know the founders named their art Kajukenbo. The big mystery is why the Kajukenbo name was not used publicly until 1957 when its first public use is found on the student admission forms for the

Kajukenbo Self-Defense Institute, Wahiawa school, and then in the local Honolulu newspaper.

What rank did the founders hold?

JOSEPH HOLCK

On March 3, 2021, I conducted an interview with Barry Holck, Joseph Holck's son. I learned when the founders began training together in 1947, Holck was the only known member of the group to hold a martial arts rank. He had a brown belt in Danzan Ryu jujitsu. On July 14, 1948, Henry Okazaki and Sig Kufferath promoted Holck to the rank of Shodan, black belt, 1st degree, making Holck the first member of the group to achieve the rank of black belt. In 1949, Holck received the rank of Nidan, black belt, 2nd degree, from Henry Okazaki and Sig Kufferath and his certificate of mastery (Kaidensho) and his instructor's scroll (Mokuruku), making Holck a certified martial arts master.

ADRIANO EMPERADO

When the founders began training together in 1947, Emperado did not yet have any martial arts rank. In 1949, Emperado became Chow's first student to be promoted to the rank of Shodan, black belt, 1st degree, in kenpo jiu-jitsu (Haines, *Karate and its Development in Hawaii to 1959*) and (Emperado's memoirs), making Emperado the only other member of the group to receive a promotion to the rank of black belt from an outside instructor during the founding period.

PETER CHOO, FRANK ORDONEZ, AND GEORGE CHANG

There are no known records or photographs of Choo, Ordonez, or Chang receiving any martial arts rank from an outside instructor before or during the 1947-1949 founding period. The photograph of Choo taken by Ordonez in the summer of 1948 shows Choo was still a white belt at that time.

Although Choo and Ordonez had no known martial arts rank, they did have martial arts training and boxing skills, especially Choo who would have participated in approximately 80 ring fights by the time the founders began training together based on the ring record Choo provided in the *Stars & Stripes* military article dated Aug 12, 1953, and the numerous newspaper articles chronicling his 12-year amateur boxing career.

When did the founders create the Black Belt Society?

In the Tucson interview, Emperado talks about the Black Belt Society. He said when the founders first got together in 1947 that was the beginning of the Black Belt Society but then Emperado went on to say the Black Belt Society was not actually created at that time. Holck made no comment.

Most likely, if the Black Belt Society was created by the founders, it would have been created in 1949 after Emperado received a black belt from his instructor William Chow. It doesn't seem reasonable to believe Emperado would create the Black Belt Society unless he was an actual black belt.

In researching the name Black Belt Society, I found numerous newspaper articles. All of them were judo related. The earliest article was dated March 18, 1950, and describes a judo exhibition held in Northern California featuring members of the Judo Black Belt Society. A January 22, 1955, newspaper article that I located features a judo practitioner named Charles Swan who received his second degree (nidan) promotion from the Kodokan Judo Institute in Tokyo, Japan. The article states Swan's promotion into the Black Belt Society qualifies him as an instructor under Japanese collegiate and AAU rules. Other articles from the 1950s that use the Black Belt Society name feature judo schools on the East Coast and the Midwest. So, the use of the name Black Belt Society by judo schools in the United States in the 1950s was prevalent.

Emperado and Holck both trained in Kodokan judo. Emperado with Sensei Taneo before the Kajukenbo founders got together in 1947, and Holck with Sensei Inouye starting in 1948, while the founders were training together. Either one may have heard the

Black Belt Society name being used through their association with judo and adopted it as their own.

Emperado has often repeated that the founders created the Black Belt Society. When Holck moved to Tucson in the 1960s, he established an organization he named the Kodenkan Yudanshakai, which is translated as "School of ancient traditions, Black Belt Society." So, both maintained an association with the Black Belt Society name. However, there are no known documents, articles or photographs from the 1947 – 1949 founding period of Kajukenbo showing the establishment of the Black Belt Society. The only evidence that the founders used the Black Belt Society name for their organization is Emperado's word.

Were Choo, Ordonez, and Chang promoted to black belts?

Emperado has routinely claimed the founders were all black belts. Research shows that only Holck and Emperado have records of promotion to the rank of black belt from their instructor during the founding period. Since there are no known sources to show Choo, Ordonez, and Chang earned a black belt from an outside instructor, an option may be that they were promoted by the Black Belt Society.

In the Tucson interview Emperado said Ordonez's mother created all their uniforms and sewed their black belts. Why would she do that? There needed to be a reason for Ordonez's mother to make each of the founders a uniform and a black belt. Was the reason, the founding of the Black Belt Society by Emperado and Holck? Did they promote Choo, Ordonez, and Chang to black belt? Clearly all speculation, but an option.

The Kajukenbo founders created techniques of their own, gave their art the name Kajukenbo, and according to Emperado established an organization of their own which they called the Black Belt Society. Unfortunately, commitments to the military caused them to disband before they could move forward and possibly start their own school or class. Given all that the founders did it makes sense that they may have wanted to recognize all five of them as black belts. In addition, Holck was a certified 2nd degree martial arts master, so he probably had the authority to make black belt promotions if he wanted to.

If the Black Belt Society did promote Choo, Ordonez, and Chang to the rank of black belt then Emperado's claim that all the founders were black belts would be true, but currently there is just no proof that happened.

When did the founders stop training together?

Bishop states the founders stopped training together as a group in 1949 when Choo and Holck transferred from Hawaii in anticipation of the Korean War with Choo heading to Korea and Holck to the mainland. In addition, Chang enlisted in the Marine Corps Reserves and ended up in Korea. In the Tucson interview Holck added that his transfer from Hawaii in 1949 occurred when he went to Ft. Benning, Georgia for infantry training.

In a newspaper review of Choo's boxing matches, Choo fought regularly in Hawaii in 1944, 1945, 1946, and 1947, but has no documented fights in Hawaii in 1948 and none in Hawaii in 1949 until December of that year, suggesting Choo's military commitments may have been extensive.

Summarizing the founding of Kajukenbo (1947 -1949)

In 1947, Frank Ordonez and Peter Choo organized a training session with their friends Adriano Emperado, Joseph Holck, and George Chang. At that time none of the five men were martial arts masters. In fact, Holck was the only person with any rank. He had a brown belt. They trained together briefly in 1947 and then continued to train together in 1948 and 1949. The training sessions were held secretly at Choo's family home in Damon Tract, at Kaheka gym, and at a military barracks in Halawa Veteran's housing that had been abandoned. During the training sessions the founders combined their various martial arts and fighting knowledge together to create some self-defense techniques.

In 1948, Holck earned a black belt in Danzan Ryu jujitsu, making Holck the first black belt in the group. In 1949, Holck was then promoted to black belt, 2nd degree, and awarded an instructor's certificate in Danzan Ryu jujitsu. Also in 1949, Emperado earned a black belt in kenpo jiu-jitsu, making Emperado the only other person from the group known to be promoted to black belt by an outside instructor through 1949.

During their time together the founders created the name Kajukenbo by combining the letters KA from karate, JU from judo and jujitsu, KEN from kenpo, and BO from boxing (Western and Chinese styles). While Choo claims to have created the name in 1947, both Holck and Emperado agreed Holck created the Kajukenbo name in 1948 or even as late as 1949. Additionally, according to Emperado the founders created their own organization which they named the Black Belt Society but disbanded because of commitments related to the Korean War.

While none of the founders were martial arts masters when the group first began training together in 1947, or even black belts, Holck and Emperado continued to train with their instructors and by 1949 Holck became a certified master of Danzan Ryu jujitsu and Emperado became a black belt in kenpo jiu-jitsu. That made Emperado one of only a few kenpo black belts in all of Hawaii, which should have been enough for him to be considered a martial arts master in 1949.

If the Black Belt Society promoted Choo, Ordonez, and Chang to black belt then the three of them could have also been considered martial arts masters, but in the martial art of Kajukenbo, not Tang Soo Do for Choo, Seikeno Ryu jujitsu for Ordonez, or Sil Lum kung fu for Chang as often reported.

Since there is no evidence to support the Black Belt Society or anyone else promoted Choo, Ordonez, or Chang to black belt, it becomes reasonable to believe only Holck and Emperado could have been considered martial arts masters during the 1947-1949 founding period of Kajukenbo.

Chapter 5

EMPERADO CONTINUES KAJUKENBO

Adriano Emperado

While we know Emperado, Holck, Choo, Ordonez, and Chang founded Kajukenbo in 1947, and then went on to create self-defense techniques of their own and establish the name Kajukenbo, a lot still needed to be done before Kajukenbo was presented to the public as a martial art. In fact, records show the name was not made public until the later part of 1957, a decade after the founders began training together. The person responsible for continuing the development of Kajukenbo after the founders disbanded was Adriano Emperado.

Emperado's first group of students

From Bishop's book and the Panther interview featuring Emperado and Gary Forbach, Emperado said in 1949, he began training his first group of students at Halawa Veteran's Housing. The group consisted of ten students and included Emperado's brother Joe, Marino Tiwanak, who was a retired former professional boxer, Vernon Chong, Walter Lee, Ben Lau, Stanley Machida, Machida's nephew, and three others. It is unknown if Emperado began training his students before the Kajukenbo founders disbanded or after, but nonetheless this was Emperado's first group of students.

Chow promotes Emperado to black belt, 5th degree

Even though Emperado was teaching his own students, he continued to train from Chow, as did his brother Joe. In the Panther interview Emperado explains that in the 1950s Chow promoted Emperado to the rank of black belt, 5th degree. Emperado added during that time he and his brother Joe would go to the Nuuanu Y.M.C.A. where Chow had his school and assist Chow in teaching classes.

Emperado receives an Instructor Certificate

James Mitose

Bishop tells us that in 1951, Emperado received private lessons from Professor James Mitose at Mitose's home. The extent of those lessons is not known but after the lessons Mitose presented Emperado with an Instructor's Certificate. That would have made Emperado only one of the few martial artists ever certified to teach kenpo jiu-jitsu under Mitose.

Emperado moves to the Palama Settlement

810 N Vineyard Blvd, Honolulu, Hawaii

The exact year Emperado moved his group from Halawa Veteran's Housing to the Palama Settlement gym is debatable. Emperado has routinely said the group moved to the Palama Settlement in 1950, including in the Panther interview, but author Bruce Haines completed a thesis at the University of Hawaii called *Karate and its Development in Hawaii to 1959*, and in doing so interviewed the Program Director at Palama Settlement, Mr. Lorin Gill, on May 23, 1962. According to Gill, the official records show Emperado began teaching formal classes at the Palama Settlement gym in May of 1952. The thesis

Haines completed became the book *Karate's History and Traditions* published in 1968.

Over the years others have talked about training with Emperado at the Palama Settlement gym as early as 1950 including Walter Lee. One consideration is that James Mitose, Thomas Young, and Woodrow McCandless all taught classes there. Perhaps Emperado used their space to teach his classes. Then in May of 1952, Emperado's classes were added to the formal schedule.

Emperado's second group of students

Joe Emperado, Adriano Emperado, Woodrow McCandless

In the Panther interview, Emperado said he was unaware that his brother Joe was privately teaching a group of students on the side. According to Emperado, Joe had a blue/green belt in kenpo under Chow at the time and was teaching students of his own at home. Those students included Ben Kekumu, Benny Madiro, and Mansfield Cuarisma, all prominent martial artists in later years. Emperado said all of Joe's students became part of Emperado's second group of students (The first group being the Halawa group).

Joe Emperado was awarded a black belt in 1952, so that helps us date Emperado's second group of students to 1951 or 1952 but before Joe Emperado's promotion in that year. It's estimated that John Leoning also began training from Emperado at about the same time, transferring his training from Chow's school to Emperado's.

Emperado added in the Panther interview that Woodrow McCandless, a black belt under Mitose and Young, became part of Emperado's second group of students. Emperado said McCandless watched him teach at Palama Settlement and asked Emperado if he could learn. Emperado said, "No fool around Mac, you're more advance than me," but McCandless was serious and "got in line" with Emperado's other students and joined the class, staying with Emperado until McCandless died in December of 1956.

Emperado promotes first black belt

According to Bishop, in 1952, Emperado promoted his brother Joe to the rank of Shodan, black belt, 1st degree, making Joe Emperado the first student under Emperado to reach the level of black belt. In the Panther interview, Emperado said after they formed their own school, he and his brother Joe continued to train from Chow and teach classes for Chow.

I located a newspaper article dated November 17, 1952, that shows Joe Emperado was still actively training with Chow. In the article Joe Emperado is preparing to assist Chow in doing a demonstration at Nuuanu Y.M.C.A. along with Manuel Dela Cruz, Edward Bobby Lowe, Paul Yamaguchi, and Herman Kamauni. In the newspaper photo Joe Emperado is wearing a dark color belt which may confirm his status as a black belt in 1952.

Joe Emperado at Palama Settlement gym

Joe Emperado striking the makiwara

Mitose visits Emperado's school

In the Emperado Speaks interview, Emperado told Bishop that in 1953, James Mitose, Arthur Keawe, and Masaichi Oshiro went to Emperado's class at the Palama Settlement gym. Oshiro demonstrated the martial arts form Naihanchi. Afterward, Emperado's group demonstrated their techniques. Mitose told Emperado he should call his art kenpo jiu jitsu because that was the root of Emperado's martial art. Emperado told Mitose he could not do that because the techniques were created by the five Kajukenbo creators. Hearing that, Mitose became enraged and told Emperado he would come back the next day with a samurai sword and kill Emperado. The next day passed but Mitose did not return.

A lot can be derived out of a story like that, but I think what is most important is knowing that even though Emperado was a student of Chow and an assistant instructor who taught for Chow, Emperado continued to teach the techniques that were created by the five Kajukenbo founders and acknowledged where the techniques came from to Mitose and others.

Seronio joins the Palama school

George Seronio and Adriano Emperado

By the end of 1953, George "Pauly" Seronio had completed a brief amateur boxing career and began training under Emperado at the Palama Settlement gym. Seronio attended grade school with Joe Emperado and in his younger years lived with the Emperado family. Seronio would eventually teach at the Palama, Wahiawa, Kaimuki, and Hilo schools, and become one of Emperado's earliest black belts and Kajukenbo instructors.

Emperado adds martial arts forms to Kajukenbo

It's projected that Emperado, and his brother Joe began creating and adding martial arts forms to their kenpo style around 1954 or 1955. That's based off documents found after Emperado passed away on April 4, 2009, by Emperado's nephew and Chief of the Kajukenbo Self-Defense Institute, Jim "Kimo" Emperado Smith and Deputy Chief Glen Fraticelli. The documents have the heading *Palama Settlement Exercises* on them and the written descriptions match the movements of the Emperado-Method forms.

The finalized curriculum for Kajukenbo in the late 1950s to early 1960s contains 14 martial arts forms. In discussing the development of the forms with Bishop, Emperado credits his brother Joe with creating two of them, which are numbered 4 and 7 in the Kajukenbo curriculum. Emperado said he created the remaining 12 forms himself. When naming the forms, Emperado called them pinans because he thought pinans was the Asian name for martial arts forms.

In 1993, Emperado formally changed the name of the 14 Kajukenbo forms from pinans to Palama Sets to better reflect where the forms were created, which was the Palama Settlement gym where Emperado and his brother Joe had their first formal school.

On August 7, 2021, I interviewed James Roberts, who began training from Emperado in 1958 at the old Japanese school, which was the location for the Wahiawa Kajukenbo school before Emperado moved it to the Wahiawa Y.M.C.A. According to Roberts at that time Kajukenbo had just seven martial arts forms in its curriculum which included the traditional Okinawan forms Pinan Shodan, Pinan Nidan, Naihanchi Shodan, Naihanchi Nidan and three additional forms Emperado called basic 1, 2, and 3.

From the explanation Roberts provided about each form that Emperado taught the traditional Okinawan form Pinan Shodan was modified and adopted into the Kajukenbo curriculum as Palama Set 9 while Pinan Nidan was modified and adopted into the Kajukenbo curriculum as Palama Set 13. The traditional Okinawan form Naihanchi Shodan was modified and adopted into the Kajukenbo curriculum as Palama Set 11, but it looks like Naihanchi Nidan was discarded. As Roberts talked about the three basic forms it appears they became Palama Sets 1, 2, and 3.

The information provided by Roberts indicates that by the fall of 1958, Emperado taught forms he and Joe Emperado created as well as traditional Okinawan forms.

The following is a series of four photographs of Joe Emperado demonstrating movements from Palama Set 3 at the Palama Settlement.

Emperado promotes Marino Tiwanak

In 1955, Emperado promoted Marino Tiwanak to the rank of black belt, making Tiwanak the first student under Emperado to go from white belt to black belt. The promotion took place at Dot's Drive Inn, in Wahiawa.

Marino Tiwanak Palama Settlement circa 1955

Joe Emperado and Marino Tiwanak

Emperado's third group of students

Emperado's third group of students included Aleju Reyes at the Palama Settlement school, and Tony Ramos, Joe Black, Pedro Jerry Martin, and Richard Tokumoto, all students from the Wahiawa school. In a letter received from Emperado, he said Ramos, Black, Martin, and Tokumoto were his first group of black belts from the Wahiawa school. Emperado repeated this information in the Panther interview and said Charles Gaylord was also a student at that time training at the Kaimuki school under the direction of George Seronio.

Emperado makes additional black belt promotions

Emperado told Bishop his next group of students to earn a black belt after Joe Emperado in 1952 and Tiwanak in 1955 were Vernon Chong, Walter Lee, and Benny Madiro (His name is often spelled Mediro but newspaper records show it as Madiro). Walter Lee has since clarified that he was a brown belt, not a black belt, during his training with Emperado.

Benny Madiro shaking hands with Adriano Emperado circa 1955/56

Seronio's black belt book

When Geroge Seronio passed away he left behind a small black binder style book with his name on it. Inside the book is the inscription *Property of Instructor George Seronio, Black Belt.* The book contains sketches and information on stances, breathing, blocking with applications, a list titled *The Golden Rules in Self-Defense*, and sketches of vital points.

Seronio taught at Emperado's Palama, Wahiawa, Kaimuki, and Hilo schools in the 1950s. Emperado most likely taught this information to Seronio, and Seronio passed it on to the students he taught. The discovery of Seronio's black belt book offers an opportunity to gain a better understanding of some of the concepts and ideas that were taught at the early Kajukenbo schools and is the only known black belt book in existence from one of the original Kajukenbo instructors of the 1950s.

George Serowio

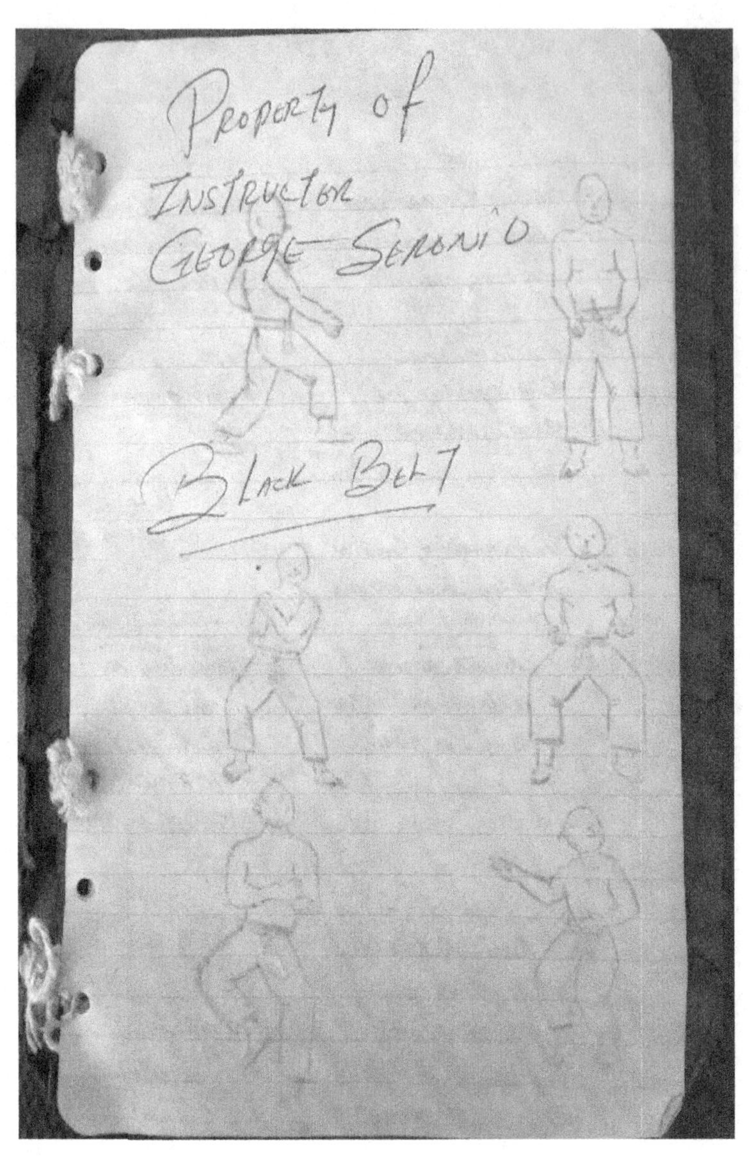
Property of
Instructor
George Seronio
Black Belt

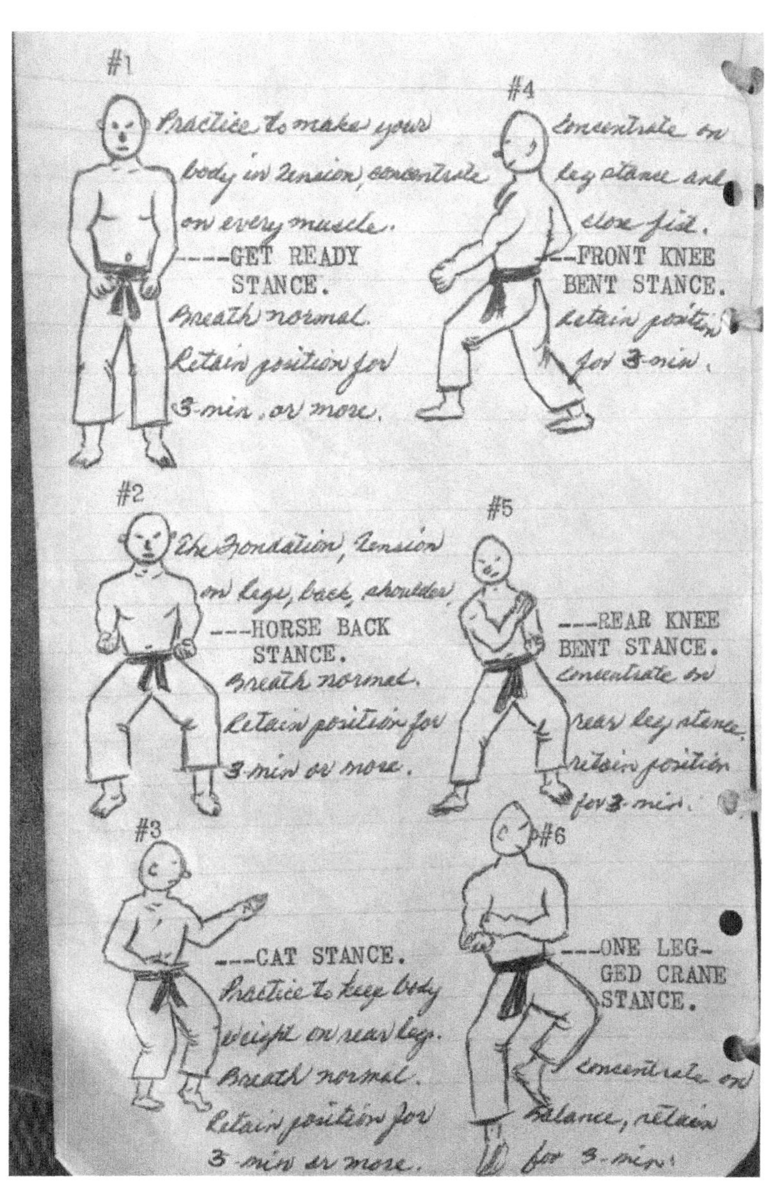
#1
Practice to make your body in tension, concentrate on every muscle.
----GET READY STANCE.
Breath normal.
Retain position for 3-min. or more.
#4
Concentrate on leg stance and close fist.
--FRONT KNEE BENT STANCE.
Retain position for 3-min.
#2
The foundation, tension on legs, back, shoulder.
---HORSE BACK STANCE.
Breath normal.
Retain position for 3-min or more.
#5
---REAR KNEE BENT STANCE.
Concentrate on rear leg stance.
Retain position for 3-min.
#3
---CAT STANCE.
Practice to keep body weight on rear leg.
Breath normal.
Retain position for 3-min or more.
#6
---ONE LEGGED CRANE STANCE.
Concentrate on balance, retain for 3-min.

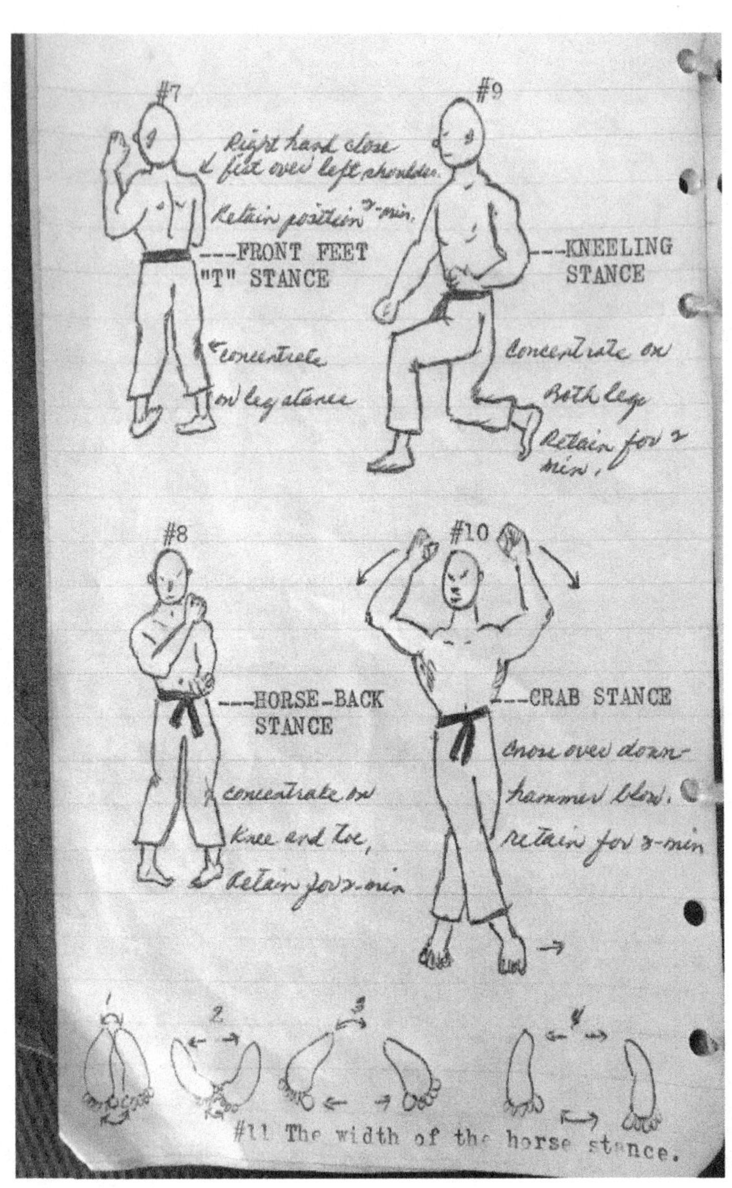

#7
Right hand close
& fist over left shoulder.
Retain position 2-min.
---FRONT FEET
"T" STANCE
concentrate
on leg stance
#9
---KNEELING
STANCE
Concentrate on
Both legs
Retain for 2
min.
#8
---HORSE-BACK
STANCE
concentrate on
Knee and Toe,
Retain for 2-min
#10
---CRAB STANCE
Cross over down
hammer blow.
retain for 2-min
1
2
3
4
#11 The width of the horse stance.

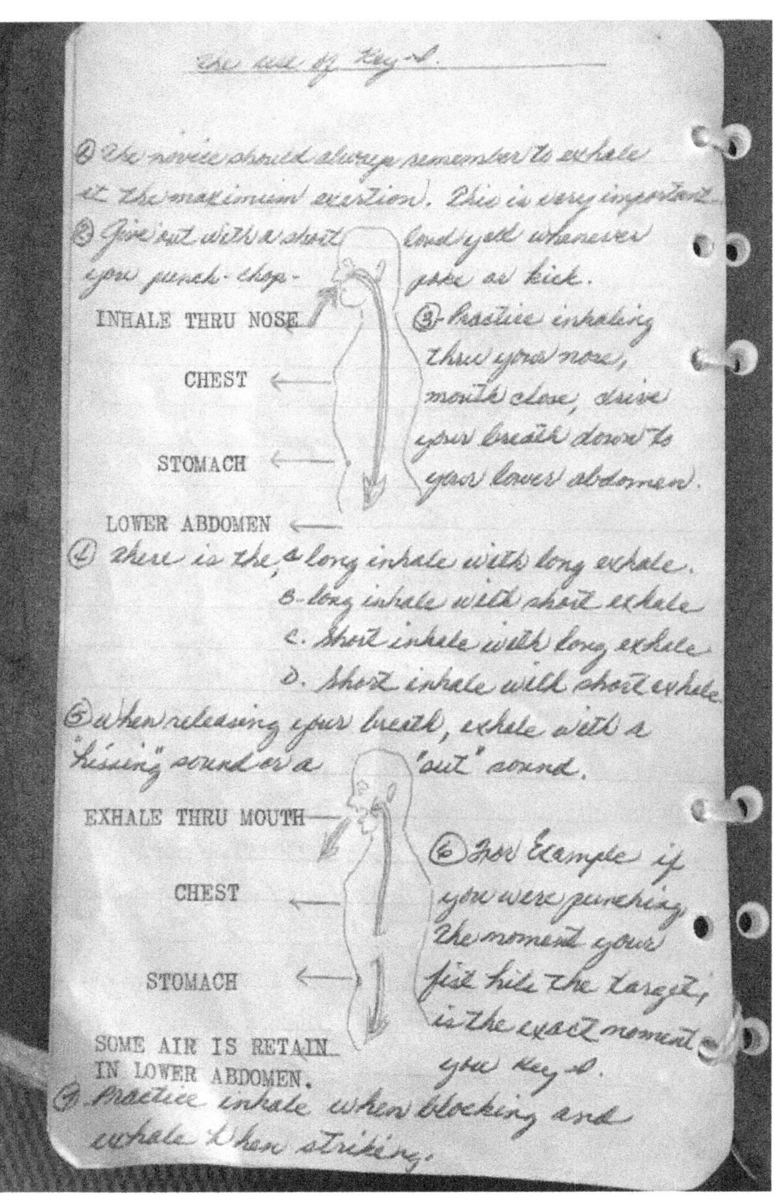

The use of Key-I.

① The novice should always remember to exhale at the maximum exertion. This is very important.

② Give out with a short loud yell whenever you punch-chop-poke or kick.

INHALE THRU NOSE

CHEST

STOMACH

LOWER ABDOMEN

③ Practice inhaling thru your nose, mouth close, drive your breath down to your lower abdomen.

④ There is the; a. long inhale with long exhale.
b. long inhale with short exhale
c. Short inhale with long exhale
d. Short inhale with short exhale.

⑤ When releasing your breath, exhale with a "hissing" sound or a "out" sound.

EXHALE THRU MOUTH

CHEST

STOMACH

SOME AIR IS RETAIN IN LOWER ABDOMEN.

⑥ For Example if you were punching, the moment your fist hits the target, is the exact moment you key-I.

⑦ Practice inhale when blocking and exhale when striking.

The Blocking Hand in the Ancient Art.

1. The block is the first step in your counter, it will protect you for an instant only, it is vitally imperative to counter almost as the same time that you've defended against his initial assault.

2. "Lin Sil, Dae Dar" this means, "As you eliminate his attack, simultaneously you begin your counterattack.

3. Certain block will make the assailant leave vital spots unguareded, which you may launch a counterattack to his low- med- or High Gates.

4. When attack more than one assailant, Count the number of opponents, Concentrate on the one closet to you.

① High wrist Block
A-3 knuckle poke to throat.
B-5 fingers poke to throat, palm facing down.
C-Hand hook to throat.
left front knee half bent.
step in punch.
② middle wrist Block
A-corkscrew punch to middle gate.
Both knees half bent.
Boxer punch stance
③ Low wrist Block
A- Right kick to low gate
Legs in horse stance.
Boxer punch stance.
Don't forget to take back step and cover.

④ Inside elbow Block.

A. Cross chop to middle gate.

Legs in horse stance

⑤ Outside elbow Block

A. Counter with horizontal elbow to middle gate.

Legs in horse stance.

⑥ Push away block

A. chop to wrist palm down.

Both legs half bent.

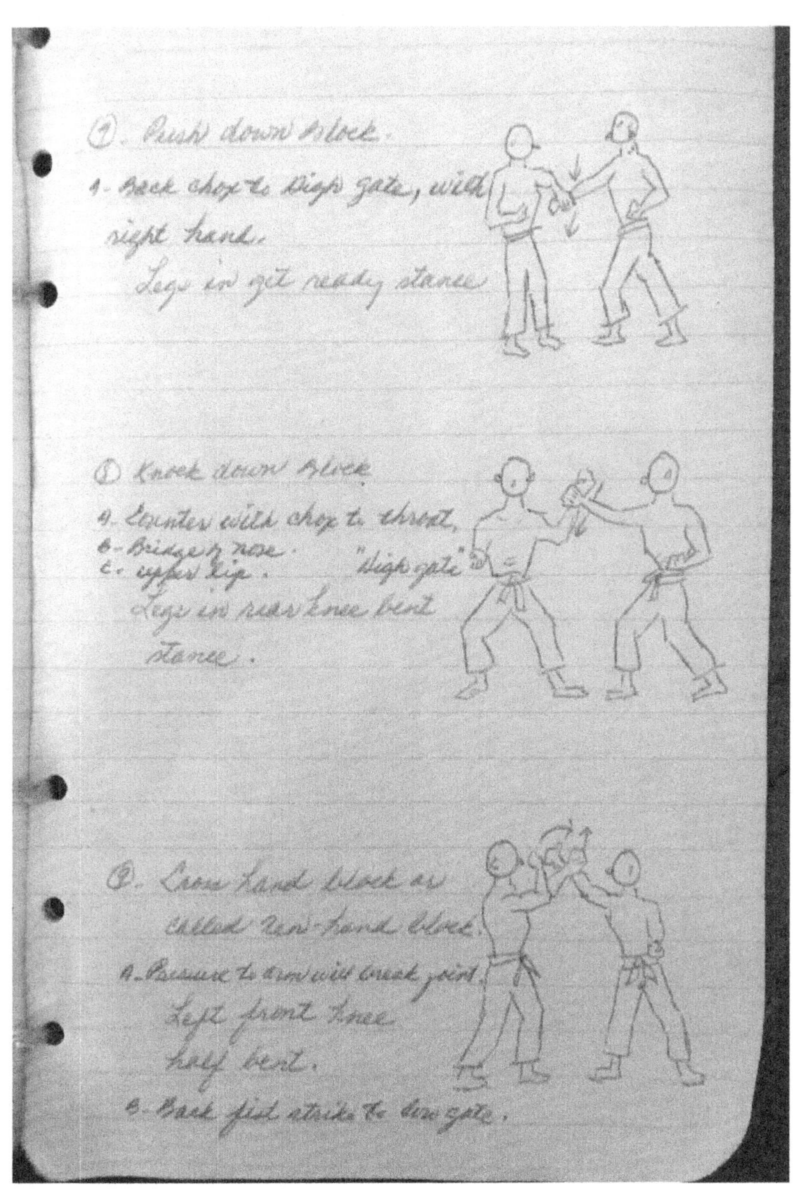

①. Push down block.

1- Back chop to high gate, with right hand.

Legs in get ready stance

② Knock down block

A- Counter with chop to throat,

B- Bridge of nose.

C- upper lip. "High gate"

Legs in rear knee bent stance.

③. Cross hand block as called Ten-hand block.

A- Pressure to arm will break joint.

Left front knee half bent.

B- Back fist strike to low gate.

(10). High chop block.
A- Counter with poke, spread, or elbow to middle gate
Legs on cat stance.

(11). middle chop Block.
A- Could be use for wrist grab, apply elbow break with other hand.
Legs on cat stance.

(12)- Low chop Block.
A- Counter with kick to low-gate,
B- Counter with Buffalo to temple;
Horse Stance.

(13) Knock away Block

A- Counter with back chop to lower-gate - groin.

Horse Stance.

B-

(14) Straight elbow blocking Horizontal elbow

(15) Horizontal elbow Blocking straight elbow.

The Golden rules in self-defense.

1. Dont ever let your body or limps get entangled. Keep them free in order to attack or defend.

2. Dont grab either their body or limbs, or clothing.

3. Dont try for holds, such as armlock, wristlock, etc. Secondary stage. Opponent must be stunned first to apply holds.

4. Garb only after block, even then, they should be of a temporary nature only, just long enough to complete your chop, punch, kick, etc.

5. Dont try any throws, wait till you've stunned attacker with a vital counter, throws maybe secondary stage.

6- Never underestimate your Assailant, Keep in mind always he too maybe well trained.

7. When you either defend or attack, Your whole body should be in back of your respective efforts, Once you've closed with the attacker, Explode with any and all natural weapons at your disposal.

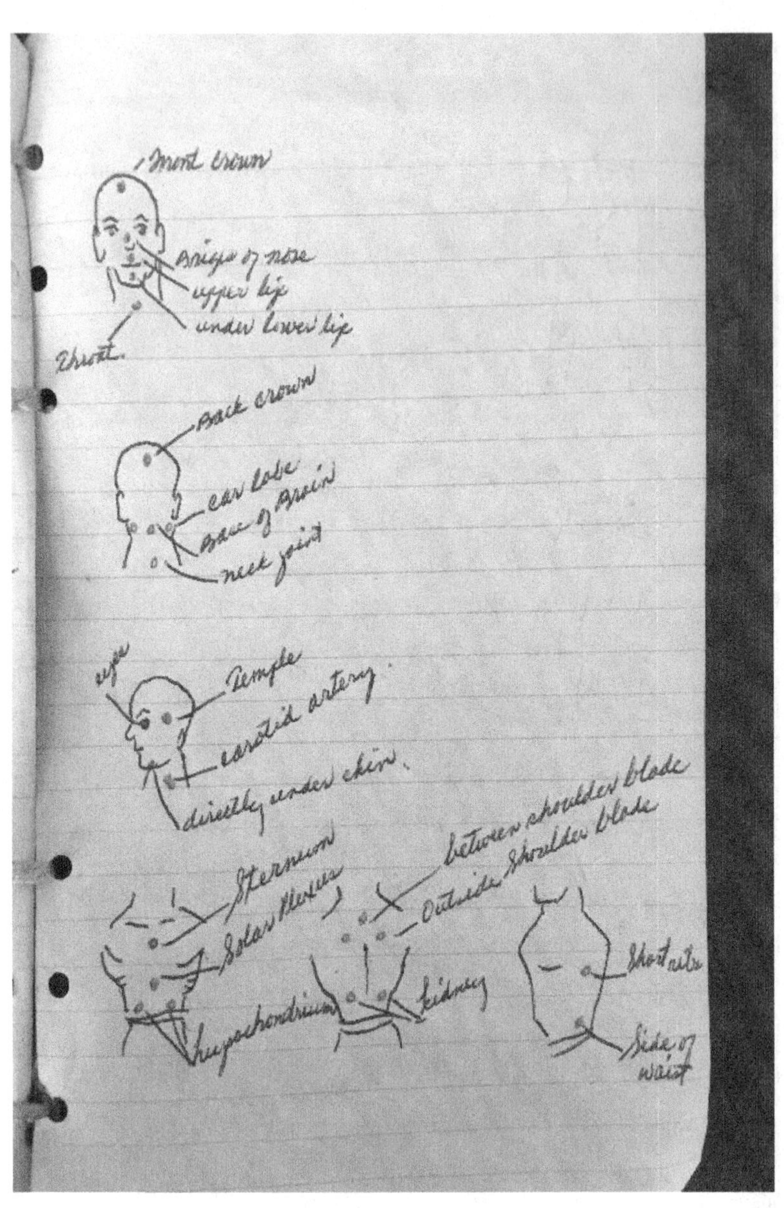
Front crown
bridge of nose
upper lip
under lower lip
Throat.
Back crown
ear lobe
Base of Brain
neck joint
eyes
Temple
carotid artery.
directly under chin.
between shoulder blade
Outside Shoulder blade
Sternum
Solar Plexus
hypochondrium
kidney
Short ribs
Side of waist

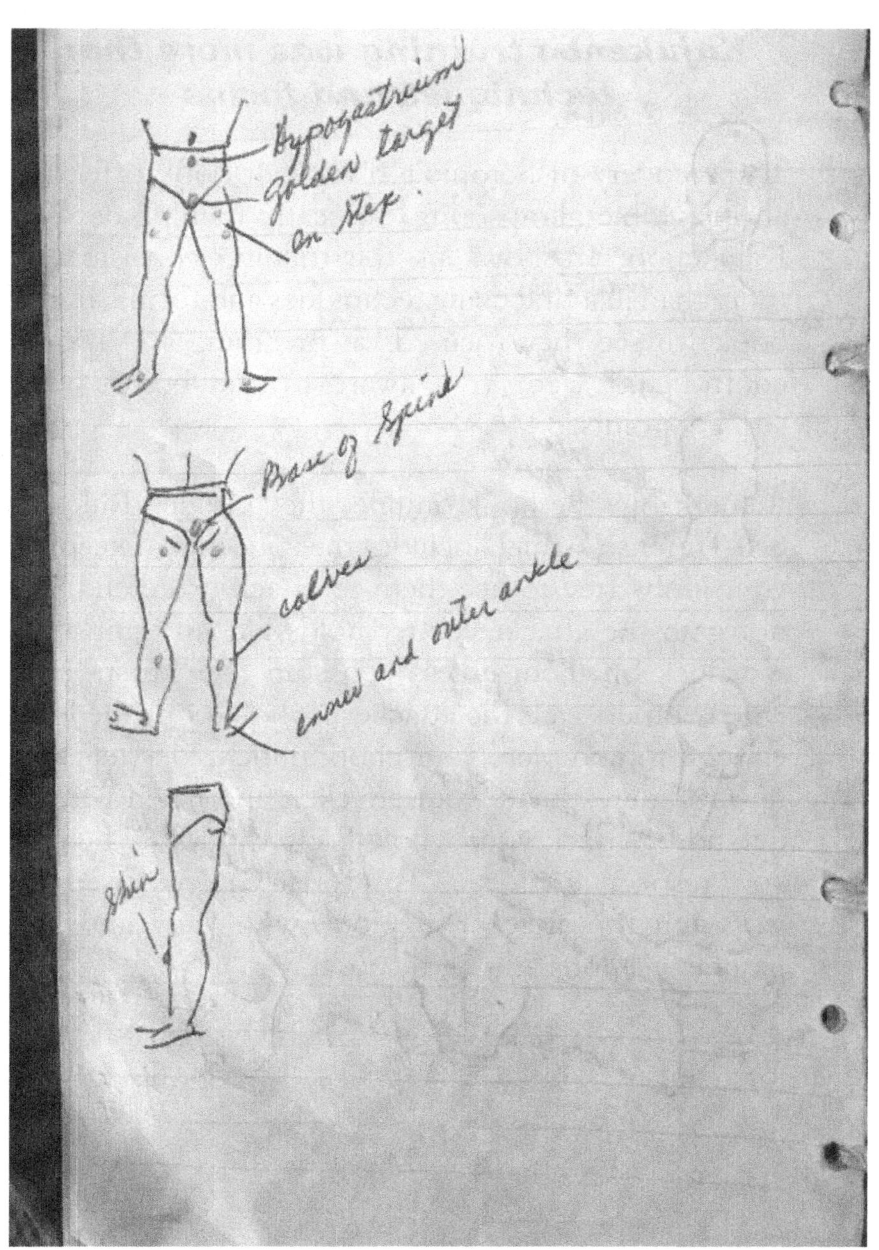
Hypogastrium
Golden target
on step
Base of Spine
calves
inner and outer ankle
shin

Kajukenbo training was more than techniques and forms

The recovery of Seronio's black belt book offers us an incredible glimpse into the early training days of Kajukenbo. It shows us the training consisted of more than just practicing techniques and forms. In the book we see they focused on breathing and breath control and were very aware of the body's vital striking points.

Remarkably, the book outlines the "Golden Rules in Self-Defense" which includes the concepts of keeping your limbs free to use them to attack or defend. To not grab the attacker or try holds like an armbar or wristlock on them unless you stun them first. That when you do grab the attacker it should only be long enough to complete your chop, punch, kick, etc. To never underestimate your attacker, and when you do defend or attack your whole body should be behind your respective efforts. Lastly, once you've closed the gap with the attacker, explode with "any and all" natural weapons at your disposal.

Chapter 6

EMPERADO'S FIRST SCHOOLS

In the Panther interview, Emperado provided details about his first three schools stating the Palama Settlement school was first followed by the Wahiawa school and then the Kaimuki school. Newspaper articles from 1957 show the Palama and Wahiawa schools were kenpo schools first under Emperado before they became Kajukenbo schools in the later part of 1957. I believe the same may be true for the Kaimuki school as well.

PALAMA SETTLEMENT SCHOOL

Tiwanak, McCandless, Adriano Emperado and Joe Emperado are seated in the middle

WAHIAWA Y.M.C.A. SCHOOL

Frank Ordonez, Adriano Emperado and Joe Emperado (Black uniforms) and Tony Ramos (Front row center)

KAIMUKI Y.M.C.A. SCHOOL

Charles Gaylord was a student of Seronio at the Kaimuki school

KALIHI SCHOOL

John Kanehailua

John Pascua

On November 26, 2020, Albert Saddler coordinated an interview that was conducted with John Kanehailua, who said, in 1957, John Leoning established the Kalihi school and recruited John's brother James, and a friend of James' named Phillip Somera. They became Leoning's first students and then later John Kanehailua and others like John Pascua joined the school.

Kanehailua provided photos of himself, and John Pascua as white belt students dressed in their class uniform. The photos show a makiwara in the background, a common training tool handed down from the Mitose era and used by the Chow and Emperado groups. Also notice Kanehailua and Pascua are wearing the round Emperado-Method Kajukenbo patch.

Emperado school instructors

Bishop states that Joe Emperado emerged as the primary teacher at the Palama Settlement school when Adriano Emperado began teaching at the Y.M.C.A. schools. Emperado added in the Panther interview that Seronio taught at both the Wahiawa and Kaimuki schools.

A newspaper article from the Honolulu Star Bulletin dated Nov 27, 1957, and titled, "Kenpo Club Seeks Queen Contestants for Benefit Dance," states the Palama-Wahiawa Kenpo Club is sponsoring the dance and then it lists the instructors for Emperado's schools. Adriano "Sonny" Emperado, Joe Emperado, and Marino Tiwanak are listed as the instructors for the Palama Settlement school, and George P. Seronio is listed as the instructor for the Wahiawa school.

From documents obtained following the death of George Seronio we know Tony Ramos was Seronio's assistant at the Wahiawa school. In the Panther interview Emperado said Charles Gaylord was Seronio's assistant at the Kaimuki school. John Kanehailua said he and his brother James were Leoning's assistants at the Kalihi school and they ran the school when Leoning left Hawaii for Los Angeles.

Chapter 7

KEMPO JIU-JITSU BECOMES KAJUKENBO

When George Seronio passed away on August 28, 2020, he left behind a box containing Kajukenbo documents and memorabilia, which included an instructor's manual, patches, and approximately forty school admission forms for the Wahiawa Kajukenbo Self-Defense Institute, where Seronio was an instructor. Those forms are currently the earliest known documents to contain the name Kajukenbo on them and the organizational name Kajukenbo Self-Defense Institute.

It is through these documents that we can establish when Kajukenbo became an official martial art. While it is known that the Kajukenbo founders created the name Kajukenbo during the 1947-1949 founding period there is no known recorded public use of the Kajukenbo name prior to its use on the Wahiawa Kajukenbo school admission forms. Given that we can project Kajukenbo became an official martial arts style at least by September of 1957. Since Kajukenbo was created in the territory of Hawaii it also became an American martial art.

The admission forms do not have "Wahiawa Kajukenbo" printed on them, so they are not exclusive to the Wahiawa Kajukenbo school. Emperado could have used them at any of his other Kajukenbo schools under the Kajukenbo Self-Defense Institute banner. The forms consist of two pages each and have the wording "Kajukenbo Self-Defense Institute," printed on page 1 and 2.

The forms are signed by Adriano Emperado as the chief instructor, Joe Emperado as the assistant instructor, and witnessed by George Seronio, John Ventura (In a few instances), and Antonio "Tony" Ramos. More importantly, the forms have handwritten dates on them beginning September 9th through the end of December of 1957.

Based on Seronio keeping the Wahiawa school admission forms his entire life they must have represented something very special to him. Some options would be the admission forms are from the time when Seronio became an instructor at the Wahiawa school, or the forms might be from the opening of the Wahiawa Kajukenbo school.

I have attached the school admission forms for Richard Tokumoto, Anthony Glushenko, and Dexter Choy. <u>All three forms are signed September 9, 1957, making these forms the earliest known Kajukenbo documents in existence.</u>

Richard Tokumoto Admission Form (Page 1)

NAME : TOKUMOTO, RICHARD
(Last Name First – PRINT)

DATE: 9/9/57

ADDRESS: 64 Kuahiwi Ave.

PHONE : 228098

I, THE UNDERSIGNED AGREE TO WAIVE ANY CLAIMS AGAINST THE:

KAJUKENBO SELF-DEFENSE INSTITUTE

AND ITS REPRESENTATIVE FOR ANY INJURIES AND/OR DEATH ARISING FROM OR RECEIVED DURING PRACTICE., OR REGULARLY SCHEDULE CLASSES, OR CONTEST.

WITNESSED BY:

Richard S. Tokumoto
(SIGNATURE)

A. Emperado
(CHIEF INSTRUCTOR)

J. Emperado
(ASST. INSTRUCTOR)

Richard Tokumoto Admission Form (Page 2)

KAJUKENBO
SELF DEFENSE INSTITUTE

QUESTION:

STATE YOUR PRIMARY AND SECONDARY REASONS FOR LEARNING THIS UNIQUE ART OF SELF-DEFENSE:

(1) Self Defense

(2) I am very much interested in the Japanese ~~way~~ art of self defense

OTHER

Richard S. Tokumoto
(NAME)

9/9/57
(DATE STARTED)

May 16, 1937 — 20
(DATE OF BIRTH) (AGE)

Anthony Glushenko's Admission Form (Page 1)

NAME : GLUSHENKO ANTHONY JR DATE: 9/9/57
(Last Name First - PRINT)

ADDRESS: 2340 C KALAUWU ST

PHONE : 846 842

I, THE UNDERSIGN AGREE TO WAIVE ANY CLAIMS AGAINST THE:

KAJUKENBO SELF-DEFENSE INSTITUTE

AND ITS REPRESENTATIVE FOR ANY INJURIES AND/OR DEATH ARISING FROM OR RECEIVED DURING PRACTICE., OR REGULARLY SCHEDULE CLASSES, OR CONTEST.

WITNESSED BY:

George Lesonio

[illegible]

[illegible]

Anthony Glushenko Jr
(SIGNATURE)

A. Emperado
(CHIEF INSTRUCTOR)

J. Emperado
(ASS'T. INSTRUCTOR)

Anthony Glushenko Admission Form (Page 2)

KAJUKENBO
SELF DEFENSE INSTITUTE

QUESTION:

STATE YOUR PRIMARY AND SECONDARY REASONS FOR LEARNING THIS UNIQUE ART OF SELF-DEFENSE:

(1) Self defense

(2) I have been interested in the Japanese custom of Self defense for a long time

OTHER

Anthony Glushenko Jr.
(NAME)

9/1/57
(DATE STARTED)

4-7-36 21
(DATE OF BIRTH) (AGE)

Dexter Choy's Admission Form (Page 1)

NAME : Choy, Dexter (Last Name First - PRINT)   DATE: 9/9/57

ADDRESS: P.O. Box 478 WAH.

PHONE : 225092

I, THE UNDERSIGN AGREE TO WAIVE ANY CLAIMS AGAINST THE:

KAJUKENBO SELF-DEFENSE INSTITUTE

AND ITS REPRESENTATIVE FOR ANY INJURIES AND/OR DEATH ARISING FROM OR RECEIVED DURING PRACTICE., OR REGULARLY SCHEDULE CLASSES, OR CONTEST.

WITNESSED BY: Dexter K. Choy (SIGNATURE)

[illegible]

[illegible]

[illegible]

A. Emperado
(CHIEF INSTRUCTOR)

J. Emperado
(ASS'T INSTRUCTOR)

Dexter Choy Admission Form (Page 2)

KAJUKENBO
SELF DEFENSE INSTITUTE

QUESTION:

STATE YOUR PRIMARY AND SECONDARY REASONS FOR LEARNING THIS UNIQUE ART OF SELF-DEFENSE:

(1) Self-Defense

(2) To Learn and Give My Self An Improve Art Kaju Ken Bo

OTHER

Dexter K. Choy
(NAME)

9/9/57
(DATE STARTED)

4/8/37 19
(DATE OF BIRTH) (AGE)

Future Wahiawa Kajukenbo black belts

Besides the form for Tokumoto, the collection includes admission forms for Pedro Jerry Martin, Raymond Chun, and Curtis Arrayan. Tokumoto, Martin, and Chun were all promoted to black belt by Emperado and Arrayan went on to spend the remainder of his life training and teaching Kajukenbo.

Did women and kids train in Kajukenbo?

For years I was told women and children did not train in Kajukenbo in the early days. The Wahiawa school was the second school founded by Emperado and based on the discovery of the Wahiawa Kajukenbo admission forms was established at least by September 9, 1957. The admission forms address the question about women and kids training in Kajukenbo. While the forms do not have a place on them to list the sex of the applicant at least three of the forms have what I would consider a female name and six of the forms list birthdates showing the applicant was under 18 years old.

There are forms with the first names of Courtney, Ilima, and Melva. When Ilima and Melva listed the reason for taking the class they both wrote that they were female. While these forms do not address women training at the other Emperado schools, they do show women trained at the Wahiawa Kajukenbo school.

An admission form for a student named Raymond Hamamoto included a letter from his mother granting Hamamoto permission to take classes. Hamamoto joined on November 23, 1957, and listed his age as 16 years old. The forms for Roy Ogasawara, Paul Rivera, Patrick O'Hara, Leroy Paokao, and Dickie Qhiseng show all of them to be 17 years old. From that we know students under the age of 18 were allowed to train but there were no students younger than 16 years of age.

Method by "Kempo Jiu-Jitsu"

Interestingly, the school admission forms all have a stamp on them that appears to have been added to each form separately by a mechanical stamping device. The stamp reads *Kajukenbo Self-Defense Institute, Method by Kempo Jiu-Jitsu.* Research shows Mitose called his art kenpo jiu-jitsu at the time that he was teaching Emperado's instructor William Chow. Although Chow used many different names to describe the martial art he taught, he did use the kenpo jiu-jitsu name, so Emperado's use of the name is not surprising.

When doing research, you will find kenpo is sometimes spelled with an "N" and sometimes spelled with an "M." For Mitose's book *What is Self-Defense?*

Kenpo Jiu-Jitsu. Kenpo is spelled with an "N." On an advertisement in the local paper from Mar 2, 1946, Mitose announces that he is now teaching kempo along with jiu-jitsu. In that advertisement Mitose uses the "M." The spelling varied often in the early years. It is unclear why Emperado chose to use the kempo "M" spelling for the stamp on his forms.

After the Kajukenbo name started being used publicly, Emperado changed the name of his method from kempo jiu-jitsu to Emperado-Method Kajukenbo. That information is based on interviews I conducted. One with James Roberts, who began training from Emperado at the Wahiawa Kajukenbo school in 1958. I asked Roberts what patch they wore, and he described the round red and black Kajukenbo patch with the wording Emperado-Method on it. In a second interview featuring John Kanehailua, a student of the Kalihi Kajukenbo school in 1958, he said their group also wore the Emperado-Method patch and provided photos. In addition, Charles Gaylord is also photographed wearing the Emperado-Method patch as a student at Kaimuki.

The Photo above is of the stamp from the Wahiawa Kajukenbo School admission form dated September 9,1957. In a circular manner it reads *Kajukenbo* on the top and *Self-Defense Institute* on the bottom. In the center it reads *Method by Kempo Jiu-Jitsu.*

First time the Kajukenbo name appears in print

On Saturday, December 28, 1957, an article was placed in the Honolulu Advertiser titled, "Self-Defense Group Elects Officials." In the article the Kajukenbo Self-Defense Institute of Palama Settlement announces the names of people who were elected to fill positions in the organization. Adriano Emperado is the chief instructor. Joe Emperado is the assistant chief instructor. Marino Tiwanak is an instructor. Benny Kekumu, Antone Silva, Lawrence Kaowili, Charley Lee, Kosei Yamane are listed as directors. Aleju Reyes is listed as the secretary-treasurer, and Howard Paiohuli is listed as the sergeant-of-arms.

This is the first time the Kajukenbo name, and the Kajukenbo Self-Defense Institute organizational name appears in a newspaper.

Palama-Wahiawa Kenpo Club

Prior to December 28, 1957, the newspaper articles that I located for Emperado's school call the school the Palama Kenpo Club or the Palama-Wahiawa Kenpo Club. None of the articles use the Kajukenbo name or the Kajukenbo Self-Defense Institute organizational name. The last article I found using the Palama-Wahiawa Kenpo Club name for Emperado's school is dated Dec 4, 1957, from the Honolulu Advertiser and titled "Miss Red Feather of 1957' Chosen." The article explains the Palama-Wahiawa Kenpo Club sponsored the Miss Red Feather contest at the Wahiawa gym. The contest was won by Violet Kutz, a senior at Sacred Hearts Academy.

Chapter 8

THE KAJUKENBO SELF-DEFENSE INSTITUTE

The recovery of the Wahiawa Kajukenbo school admission forms and the dates attached to them allow us to project 1957 as not only the date when the name Kajukenbo began to be used publicly but also the date when the organizational name of the Kajukenbo Self-Defense Institute began being used publicly. Emperado may have used the names earlier but there are no known records to show that.

The article in the Honolulu Advertiser dated December 28, 1957, supports the documents found from the Wahiawa Kajukenbo school showing the Kajukenbo name and the Kajukenbo Self-Defense Institute name being used publicly for the first time in 1957.

On November 26, 1996, Robert "Twinkle" Kawakami passed away. He was 74 years old. In his obituary Kawakami is listed as the co-founder of the Kajukenbo Self-Defense Institute. Research suggests that Ordonez introduced Kawakami to Emperado and Kawakami became instrumental in the expansion of Emperado's schools. That information and Kawakami's obituary would place Emperado's connection to Kawakami to at least 1957, when the Kajukenbo Self-Defense Institute name surfaced, and when Emperado began using the name Kajukenbo and adding schools.

In April of 1968, Kawakami became the Chairman of the Kajukenbo Self-Defense Institute governing board. A board that took on the responsibility of promoting Emperado to the rank of 10th degree in the art of Kajukenbo and awarding him the title of professor. The action by the KSDI board took place shortly after the Chinese Hawaiian Physical Culture Association promoted Emperado to 10th degree in the art of kenpo and awarded Emperado the title of professor. The 1968 date establishes a relationship of more than a decade between Kawakami, Emperado, and Kajukenbo.

Research indicates Kawakami held various roles throughout his life. He was a politician, businessman, co-founder of the Kajukenbo Self-Defense Institute, and he was a musician, which is where he got his nickname "Twinkle." That came from the name of his band Twinkle & His Little Stars. Newspaper articles from 1941 feature an amateur boxer named Robert Kawakami who fought as a flyweight for the Citywide boxing club. He may have been a boxer as well.

Stories have been shared over the years about Kawakami's connection with the Kajukenbo Self-Defense Institute. Many about his role in making high ranking Kajukenbo promotions for some of Kajukenbo's early pioneers. One thing is certain, Emperado gave Kawakami an abundance of power.

Chapter 9

KAJUKENBO'S FIRST PATCHES

When George Seronio was alive, he provided some background on the first three patches that were used in the 1950s by Emperado for Kajukenbo. Those patches include the Kajukembo Karate patch, the Emperado-Method Kajukenbo Karate patch, and a patch featuring a person mimicking a stance from the traditional Okinawan form Naihanchi. The photos in this book of those three patches are photos I took of Serono's actual patches. He kept all three of them his entire life.

According to Seronio, the first patch Emperado had made to represent Kajukenbo was the round Kajukembo Karate patch featuring two black belts in white uniforms executing karate moves against each other. That means Emperado initially spelled KA-JU-KEM-BO with an "M." Since the KEM portion of the word Kajukembo represents kempo that makes sense. Remember, Emperado originally called his martial arts method kempo jiu-jitsu. We know that because it is stamped on the Wahiawa Kajukenbo school admission forms.

The Kajukembo Karate Patch

Seronio said Emperado replaced the Kajukembo Karate patch with the round red, white, and black Emperado-Method Kajukenbo Karate patch.

Emperado-Method Kajukenbo Karate Patch

When Emperado replaced the Kajukembo Karate patch with the Emperado-Method Kajukenbo Karate patch, he began spelling Kajukenbo on the school patches with an 'N." The use of the "N" on the patches appears to have started sometime around 1958. I determined that based on information from James Roberts of the Wahiawa school and John Kanahailua of the Kalihi school, who both began training in Kajukenbo around 1958 and said their schools wore the Emperado-Method Kajukenbo Karate patch.

Seronio said the patch featuring the person mimicking a stance from the traditional Okinawan form Naihanchi was the instructor patch for the Wahiawa school. Photographs at Joe Emperado's funeral show Seronio and Tony Ramos both wearing the patch.

Wahiawa Instructor Patch

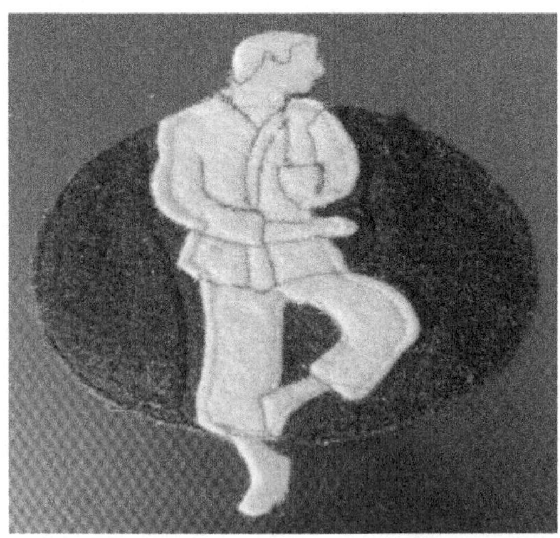

Kajukenbo and Mas Oyama

Mas Oyama and Frank Ordonez

Through Bruce Haines, we learn Edward "Bobby" Lowe received his black belt from Mitose in 1953. In 1957, Lowe began corresponding with Mas Oyama with the idea of establishing a relationship with Oyama's Japanese school. On November 15, 1958, Lowe's school officially became affiliated with Oyama's Tokyo Kyokushinkai school. The relationship Lowe development with Oyama brought Oyama to Hawaii and from there Ordonez and Emperado met Oyama and created a friendship.

The white, red, and black Palama Settlement patch that has been in circulation for years is a smaller version of the original patch. There are photos of the original patch being circulated with the date of 1955 written on the photos, but Henry Mandac, one of Emperado's black belts who began training from Emperado in the 1950s, said the original patch was actually created in 1959, not 1955.

In 1957, Mas Oyama published a book in Japan titled *What is Karate?* By 1958, the book was available in the U.S. The original cover of Oyama's book looks very familiar to Kajukenbo practitioners because the Palama Settlement patch is a replica of Oyama's first edition book cover. I was told Emperado had great respect for Mas Oyama. This could be a sign of that.

Palama Settlement Patch

Oyama Book Cover

Chapter 10

JOE EMPERADO PASSES AWAY

Through the excellent research done by David Tavares in his book *Black Robe, The Kempo/Kajukenbo Connection*, we know on May 29th, 1958, at about 9:30 -10:00 pm, Walter Godin met Joe Emperado at the Pink Elephant Bar, 367 N. Beretania Street. Around 1:30 am on May 30th, George Shimibuku, Thomas Miura, and William Sagolili entered the bar and sat at a table. Shortly afterwards Godin and Shimibuku had words, but Emperado walked over and made them shake hands. After the bar closed at about 2:10 am, Godin and Shimibuku began to have issues again as they walked outside, and an altercation began immediately between the two of them on the sidewalk in front of the bar. Emperado, Miura, and Sagolili soon joined in.

During the altercation Shimibuku removed a knife from his pocket that he was holding in his hand and stabbed Emperado multiple times in the back, chest, and both arms. The fight lasted until Shimibuku, Miura, and Sagolili ran off and then left in a car. After the incident ended Emperado went next door to the

Rosario café to wash the blood away and then he went home.

At 4:10 am, Emperado was admitted to St. Francis Hospital. Surgery was performed but at 10:25 am, Emperado died. He was just 28 years old.

The Funeral services were held at St. Theresa's Church on Wednesday, June 4th at 9 am. That was followed by internment at Nuuanu Memorial Park Mortuary.

It's important to note that many of the early Kajukenbo teachers considered Joe Emperado to be their primary instructor, especially those who trained directly under him at the Palama Settlement.

Joe Emperado's Funeral 1958

Chapter 11

THE KAJUKENBO PRAYER

The Kajukenbo prayer was written by Frank Ordonez in 1958 at Wake Island. It was adopted by the early Kajukenbo schools and recited before and after each class. The prayer goes as follows:

Almighty and eternal God. Protector of all who put their trust in thee. Accept the humble homage of our faith and love in thee, the one true God.

Bless our efforts to preserve the integrity of our United States. A nation founded on Christian principles. Enlighten our rules. Guide our lawmakers. Protect the sanctity of our homes.

And bless our efforts in these exercises, whose sole purpose is developing our bodies. To Keep others mindful of thy commandments.

Give us perseverance in our actions, that we may use this as a means to keep closer to you. The one true God.

In the name of thy beloved son, Jesus Christ our lord,

Amen

Chapter 12

KAJUKENBO INSTRUCTORS LEAVE HAWAII

According to Carlos Bunda, John Leoning left Hawaii in 1958 and moved to California where he began teaching Kajukenbo at a school on Sunset Blvd in Los Angeles, California. That is when Bunda became Leoning's student. Leoning's move from Hawaii to California made Leoning the first person to teach Kajukenbo outside of Hawaii.

John Bishop writes that Aleju Reyes was next to leave, moving to Carlsbad, California in 1959 and then to Northern California where he established a Kajukenbo school at Travis Air Force Base in Fairfield, California.

In 1960, Tony Ramos left Hawaii and moved to Los Angeles where he established a Kajukenbo school in Southern California with the assistance of Richard Tokumoto. In 1962, Ramos then moved to Fairfield, California and opened Tony Ramos Kajukenbo.

Joe Halbuna, Charles Gaylord, and Al Dacascos were next to leave Hawaii and open Kajukenbo schools in California.

John Leoning, Aleju Reyes, Tony Ramos, Joe Halbuna, Charles Gaylord, and Al Dacascos are all early pioneers of Kajukenbo. A great number of Kajukenbo practitioners around the world can trace their Kajukenbo lineage through one of those pioneers.

Something remarkable is that after more than sixty-five years the Leoning, Reyes, Ramos, Halbuna, Gaylord, and Dacascos Kajukenbo lineages are still active today.

KAJUKENBO PIONEERS

John Leoning

Aleju Reyes

Tony Ramos

Joe Halbuna

Charles Gaylord

Al Dacascos

Chapter 13

KAJUKENBO FOUNDERS AND CREATORS

Emperado, Holck, Choo, Ordonez, and Chang developed the concept of combining their various martial arts and fighting styles together and created Kajukenbo's first techniques. They developed the Kajukenbo name, and according to Emperado they formed the Black Belt Society.

Emperado and his brother Joe added forms to their curriculum and most likely additional techniques that were not created by the founders. Collectively they taught the first wave of Kajukenbo instructors, and during their time teaching together the martial arts style of Kajukenbo and the organization name of the Kajukenbo Self-Defense Institute was formally announced to the public. Kajukenbo schools, patches, and the Kajukenbo prayer were all added.

Given his role in founding Kajukenbo in 1947 and continuing the development of Kajukenbo after the founders disbanded in 1949, Adriano Emperado is both a founder and creator of Kajukenbo.

On July 22, 2022, the Kajukenbo Self-Defense Institute under the direction of Chief Jim "Kimo" Emperado Smith and Deputy Chief Glen Fraticelli posthumously recognized Joe Emperado as a 10th degree red/gold belt with the title of "Co-Creator" of Kajukenbo. This was based on Joe Emperado's role in creating and adding forms and most likely techniques to Kajukenbo, and for his role in teaching many of the first generation Kajukenbo instructors.

Co-Creator Not Co-Founder

It must be stressed that Joe Emperado was named Co-Creator. He was not named Co-Founder of Kajukenbo because he was not part of the 1947-1949 group that founded the art.

For historical purposes Adriano Emperado, Joseph Holck, Peter Choo, Frank Ordonez, and George Chang are the recognized Founders of Kajukenbo, and Adriano and Joe Emperado are the Creators of Kajukenbo.

Joe Emperado's Kajukenbo Co-Creator Certificate

Kajukenbo Self~Defense Institute Inc.

Certificate of Rank & Honor

Be It Known To All,

That The Emperado Kajukenbo Self~Defense Institute Inc. and the Emperado Family Council, by the authority granted from Sijo Adriano D. Emperado through the Chief Administrator SGM DeChi Emperado and her Successor GM Kimo Emperado, exercise given authority to recognize and establish the rightful position and title to Joseph D. Emperado to ensure his contributions and sacrifices are written and maintained in Kajukenbo history for all to see.

The Emperado Kajukenbo Self~Defense Institute,

Does hereby recognize:

Joseph Directo Emperado

The title and rank of: Co~Creator Kajukenbo Style of Self~Defense, 10th degree, Red & Gold Belt

It is hereby requested that all authorized Kajukenbo Ranked Individuals, Kajukenbo Self~Defense Institute Members and Affiliates, and Kajukenbo Organizations worldwide grant SGM Joseph D. Emperado all the respect as given the Kajukenbo Self~Defense Institute Worldwide.

Certified, granted and witnessed on this date by the official officers of the Kajukenbo Self~Defense Institute and the Emperado Family Council ~22nd Day of July 2022.

EMPERADO METHOD

GM Kimo Emperado KSDI Chief

GM Glen Fraticelli KSDI Deputy Chief

GM Cheyenne Corpus KSDI BOA Chair

Witnesses:

Chapter 14

THE PHILOSOPHY OF KAJUKENBO

Emperado has been quoted often saying, when he was teaching students, he wasn't happy until there was blood on the floor. He repeated that saying in the Panther interview and Bishop shares it in his book as well. In a video from several years back featuring Frank Ordonez sharing some of Kajukenbo's early techniques, Ordonez has a student push him forward and from there Ordonez does a shoulder role recovering to his feet but as he does the shoulder role, Ordonez simulates scooping up a handful of dirt from the ground and tossing the dirt in the eyes of his attacker.

Concepts like making sure there is blood on the floor and throwing dirt in your attacker's eyes are not standard in most martial arts styles or training halls and show some characteristics of Kajukenbo's early development. In the Panther interview Jennings asked Emperado what was unique about Kajukenbo? In his response Emperado said it's a combination of street fighting, throwing techniques, and then you have your ground techniques. Emperado called it a follow up combination.

Emperado explains how you stun the attacker to slow them and then attack the attacker but not attacking them with the one punch kill shot and stopping like they do in traditional martial arts styles. In Kajukenbo the attack you execute can start with the one punch kill shot but then that would be followed up with a throw or takedown and then some groundwork to make sure the attacker would not get up to attack you again. Emperado then provided a unique saying that captures the philosophy of Kajukenbo, **"You stun em, give em the works, then you finish them off."**

Chapter 15

A BETTER STORY TO TELL

For decades the story about how Kajukenbo became a martial art centered around the belief that it was created by five martial arts masters, and that each was a master of a different martial art. After years of research, where I have captured spoken content from oral interviews of the founders, located historical documents and photographs, conducted interviews with early Kajukenbo students and examined as much of the credible information as I can find about the early development of Kajukenbo, I believe it is time that the Kajukenbo community moves past the "Five Masters" story because there is a better story to tell. A more accurate story. One that is not based on romanticism but evidence.

Emperado, Holck, Choo, Ordonez, and Chang were raised in Hawaii during the great depression and dealt with unbelievable challenges. They all experienced the bombing at Pearl Harbor as teenagers. The hatred in Hawaii that followed towards Japanese was so severe that Holck's parents had to petition the court so they could change their Japanese last name from Matsuno to Holck. Following the bombing at Pearl Harbor

America joined World War II and Emperado, Holck, Choo, Ordonez, and Chang would all eventually join the army. Through good fortune they found each other and created friendships that brought the five of them together for what became the founding of Kajukenbo.

In 1947, when Emperado, Holck, Choo, Ordonez, and Chang first got together they did not start out trying to create a martial art. It was just five guys training together. As time went by Choo realized while training with some traditional martial artists that traditional movements and techniques were not enough when faced with a trained fighter like him. That was the light bulb moment, and it caused Choo to suggest to Emperado that they combine all their martial arts knowledge together and create techniques that could be used for any situation they faced.

At that time, none of the founders had any martial arts rank except for Holck, who had a brown belt in Danzan Ryu jujitsu, but they had training in multiple disciplines that included striking and grappling. They used that knowledge and began creating techniques by combining movements from karate, judo, jujitsu, kenpo, and boxing. After about two years of training together they completed their techniques and then Holck came up with a name. Holck combined the letters KA for karate, JU for judo and jujitsu, KEN for kenpo, and BO for Western and Chinese boxing styles to create the name KA-JU-KEN-BO.

Since Kajukenbo was created in the territory of Hawaii, it not only became a new martial art, but it also became an American martial art. Then according to Emperado the founders created an organization of their own called the Black Belt Society but then went their separate ways due to military commitments.

In 1949, Emperado began training a group of his own students, which included his brother Joe. While training together they also continued to train under their instructor William Chow. Within a year or so, Emperado moved his group to the Palama Settlement gym and began teaching a kenpo jiu-jitsu class there on the same mat as several other kenpo instructors including James Mitose, William Chow, Thomas Young, and Woodrow McCandless.

In the early 1950s, Chow promoted Emperado to black belt, 5th degree, and about the same time Emperado received an instructor certificate from Mitose. In 1952, Emperado found out his brother Joe was teaching students on the side. Those students included Ben Kekumu, Benny Madiro, and Mansfield Cuarisma. All of them then became part of Emperado's second group of students, and they were joined by Woodrow McCandless. In 1952, Emperado promoted his brother Joe Emperado to black belt making Joe the first black belt under Adriano

Emperado. In 1953, George Seronio joined the Palama Settlement school.

In 1954 or 1955, Emperado and his brother Joe began creating and implementing martial arts forms into their curriculum. They added forms which they created on their own and they added the traditional Okinawan forms of Naihanchi Shodan, Pinan Shodan and Pinan Nidan.

In 1955, Emperado promoted Marino Tiwanak to black belt, making Tiwanak the first student under Emperado to go from white belt to black belt. Following that promotion Emperado promoted additional black belts Vernon Chong, Benny Madiro, and possibly Walter Lee. More would follow.

By 1957, Emperado began adding additional schools at Wahiawa, Kaimuki, and Kalihi. Emperado also began working with a local businessman named Robert "Twinkle" Kawakami and together they founded the Kajukenbo Self-Defense Institute. That led to changing the name of Emperado's schools from the Palama Kenpo Club and Palama-Wahiawa Kenpo Club to the Kajukenbo Self-Defense Institute. Emperado then changed the name of his martial arts method from kempo jiu-jitsu to Kajukenbo.

In 1958, tragedy struck when Joe Emperado was killed. It was just a few months after Kajukenbo was announced to the public and became an official martial arts style. His funeral was an exceptional show of love and respect for his loss. Somehow, Adriano Emperado was able to continue the great work that he and his brother Joe did together in continuing the development of Kajukenbo and training the first group of Kajukenbo instructors.

After Joe Emperado's funeral, John Leoning left Hawaii and established the first Kajukenbo school on the mainland. He was followed by Aleju Reyes, Tony Ramos, Joe Halbuna, Charles Gaylord, and Al Dacascos, who all established Kajukenbo schools in California.

If the founders were martial arts master's when they began training together then you would expect them to create an amazing martial art. It's like watching an All-Star basketball game. You expect the players to do amazing things. They are the best of the best. But the Kajukenbo founders were not masters of any martial arts styles when they began training together. Just a brown belt and four white belts. Through hard work and perseverance Holck and Emperado would reach the master level during their time together, but they appear to be the only ones.

That is what makes this story about Kajukenbo so much more compelling and exceptional than the "Five Masters" story. The art wasn't created by five highly trained martial arts experts. It was created by five men surrounded by poverty, death and war and raised during some very tough times. They all began training at a young age and lived in rough and tumble areas. All five completed military training and some were still active military while training together.

The founders were aware of the challenges they would face in the street both from a striking and a grappling perspective because several of them cross-trained in multiple disciplines. With their military training they also knew what to expect in combat situations—like fighting someone with a weapon. That's the knowledge the founders drew from when creating their techniques.

As a lifelong Kajukenbo practitioner I can tell you the techniques the founders and creators implemented into the art are elementary in nature. There is nothing fancy about them. The defensive movements use basics karate blocks to stop the attack. The follow-up strikes and kicks are direct and focused on vital targets. The takedowns are the most basic applications of judo and jujitsu like a single leg takedown, an outside leg sweep, or a shoulder throw.

The toughness and practicality of Kajukenbo's techniques comes from the street sense the founders had and the fact that they used the most basic movements of their various arts when creating their techniques. Whether the founders were limited in scope by their lack of high-level martial arts training or simply smart enough to use just the basics of each art, time has shown the founders made the right decisions because Kajukenbo's techniques are still extremely valid even after all these years.

As I stated in the first chapter the real story about how Kajukenbo became an American martial art is not the one about the five fictitious martial arts masters who created the ultimate martial art, but one about the five Hawaiian born men who grew up during some unbelievably challenging times. The five men who somehow figured out a way to train secretly and combine their striking and grappling knowledge together while still training with their instructors. The five men who somehow put into place the foundation for what would become a martial art that can now be found all around the world.

That is the real story of how Kajukenbo became an American martial art, and with Emperado's perseverance and the help of his brother Joe, they finalized the art's development, introduced Kajukenbo to the public, and trained the first wave of instructors who went out and shared Kajukenbo with the masses.

KAJUKENBO SOURCES

- KAJUKENBO, The Original Mixed Martial Arts by John Bishop
- KAJUKENBO, The Emperado Legacy by John Bishop
- WORLDKAJUKENBOVIDEOS.COM (GGM Gary Forbach)
- UKFcertified.com (United Kajukenbo Federation website)
- www.Kajukenbo.com (Christopher Reyes)
- Kajukenbo Self-Defense Institute Worldwide (Facebook)
- BLACK ROBE, The Kempo/Kajukenbo Connection by David Tavares
- SOCIAL GELO with Angelo (Podcast)

RESEARCH DOCUMENTS

Emperado army discharge, Mar 17, 1947

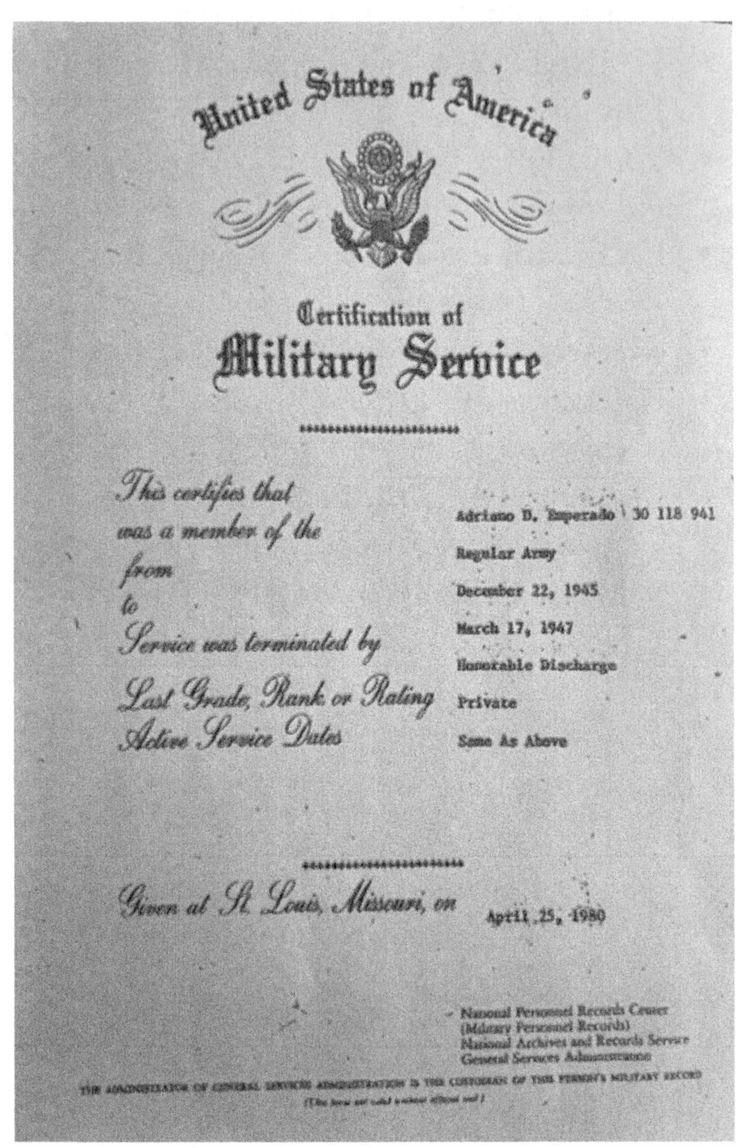

United States of America

Certification of

Military Service

This certifies that	Adriano D. Emperado 30 118 941
was a member of the	Regular Army
from	December 22, 1945
to	March 17, 1947
Service was terminated by	Honorable Discharge
Last Grade, Rank or Rating	Private
Active Service Dates	Same As Above

Given at St. Louis, Missouri, on April 25, 1980

National Personnel Records Center
(Military Personnel Records)
National Archives and Records Service
General Services Administration

THE ADMINISTRATOR OF GENERAL SERVICES ADMINISTRATION IS THE CUSTODIAN OF THIS PERSON'S MILITARY RECORD

Emperado writes about starting kenpo

My brother-in-law Woody and my sister-in-law Pauline would come over to our house in the evening and they would cook pot luck style and maybe all eat there with us. Then one night he pop up the question to me, " Nonoy, you heard of this art called Kenpo ?" So I tell him, " Kenpo, what was that ? " He say it was some kind of Okinawa Japanese self defense. He say this guy Freddie Lara and George McComba they always in front his house punching the board. So I was curious. So I say, "O, oh yea?" This guy Fredie Lara was working as security guard for Tripler Hospital. So the next day after they got through work Woody came over and picked me up and we walk over to this guy Freddie Lara house. Over there was McComba. That was in 1947. So they explained to me about what was the art about, and they was hitting the punching board to develop their knuckles. Then Fred would tell me he goes to class on Tuesdays and Thursday night if I would like to come along. I say, " Yea, I like to look." So the class

Walter Wood- The man who took Emperado to Fred Lara's house in 1947

A Piece of Kajukenbo History—The Person Responsible for Introducing Adriano Emperado to the Art of Kenpo.

By Mitch Powell

On March 17, 1947, at the age of 20, Adriano Emperado was honorably discharged from the army and back living in Hawaii at the Halawa Veteran's Housing. After speaking with his future brother-in-law, Walter "Woody" Wood Jr., Emperado learned that a friend named Fred Lara was training at Kaheka gym in Kenpo Jiu Jitsu from William Chow, a black belt student under Professor James Mitose.

One afternoon Wood walked Emperado over to Lara's residence which was just down the road from where Emperado lived. Emperado then watched Lara and George MacComber train together in the yard. Emperado was intrigued. Lara then invited Emperado to watch them train from Chow at Kaheka gym. Emperado went to the gym and watched the class. Afterward he asked Chow if he could join. Chow agreed and Emperado became one of about five white belt students training under Chow at Kaheka gym.

This information was provided by Emperado in a manuscript of a book he was writing about his life. It can be confirmed through interviews conducted by Kajukenbo historian John Bishop with Emperado prior to the writing of Bishop's book, *Kajukenbo, The Original Mixed Martial Art.*

Walter "Woody" Arthur Wood, Jr

For those interested in a deeper dive into their Kajukenbo history, I would like to introduce you to Walter "Woody" Arthur Wood, Jr. Woody married Pauline Abe, who was the sister of Emperado's wife Beatrice. Woody is the person who told Emperado about Fred Lara training in kenpo under William Chow and is the person who took Emperado to Lara's house so Emperado could see what Lara was doing. For that, the Kajukenbo world owes Walter "Woody" Arthur Wood, Jr. a debt of gratitude.

Walter "Woody" Arthur Wood, Jr. was born on October 07, 1924, and peacefully passed away on April 06, 2019, at the age of 94. He was a beloved husband, father, grandfather & great grandfather. He was survived by his loving children: Yvonne (David) Lozano, Walter III (Georgette), Scott, Kelly (Herbert) Apiag, Jr.; Six grandchildren and eight great grandchildren. He was predeceased by his wife Pauline and son Alan. Funeral services were held on Sunday, May 05, 2019, at Hawaiian Memorial Park. Visitation was at 9:30 a.m.; Services at 10:30 a.m. and a reception followed. Burial was at 1:00 p.m. at Hawaiian Memorial Park Cemetery.

Emperado heading to Guadalcanal, Oct 31, 1947

90 223

LIST OR MANIFEST OF OUTWARD-BOUND PASSENGERS (ALIENS AND CITIZENS) FOR IMMIGRATION OFFICIALS AT PORT OF DEPARTURE

Item #5

Emperado in army heading back to Hawaii, 1948

LIST OF UNITED STATES CITIZENS

(FOR THE IMMIGRATION AUTHORITIES)

Peter Choo NPRC military record

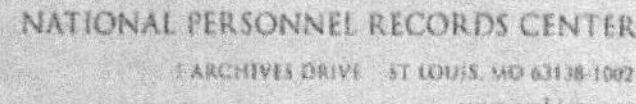

RE: Veteran's Name: CHOO, Peter Young Yil
SSN/SN: ******400
Request Number: 2-27359047125

Dear Recipient:

Thank you for contacting the National Personnel Records Center. The military service information provided in this reply has been extracted from records on file at the Center and is released to you under the Freedom of Information Act (FOIA), as amended in 1974.

Peter Y. Choo served in the U.S. Army from September 14, 1945 to September 30, 1965.

If the individual is deceased, your request must include both the written consent of the next of kin and proof of death. The next of kin is defined as: unremarried widow or widower, son, daughter, father, mother, brother or sister.

If you have questions or comments regarding this response, you may contact us at 314-801-0800 or by mail at the address shown in the letterhead above. If you contact us, please reference the Request Number listed above. If you are a veteran, or a deceased veteran's next of kin, please consider submitting your future requests online by visiting us at http://vetrecs.archives.gov.

Sincerely,

SASHANE CHIN
Archives Technician (AFN-MC5C)

We Value Our Veterans' Privacy
Let us know if we have failed to protect it.

Curtis Arrayan Wahiawa school, Nov 1957, page 1

NAME : ARRAYAN, CURTIS
(Last Name First - PRINT)

DATE: 11/57

ADDRESS:

PHONE :

I, THE UNDERSIGN AGREE TO WAIVE ANY CLAIMS AGAINST THE:

KAJUKENBO SELF-DEFENSE INSTITUTE

AND ITS REPRESENTATIVE FOR ANY INJURIES AND/OR DEATH ARISING FROM OR RECEIVED DURING PRACTICE., OR REGULARLY SCHEDULE CLASSES, OR CONTEST.

WITNESSED BY:

(SIGNATURE)

(CHIEF INSTRUCTOR)

(ASS'T. INSTRUCTOR)

Curtis Arrayan Wahiawa school, Nov 1957, page 2

KAJUKENBO
SELF DEFENSE INSTITUTE

QUESTION:

STATE YOUR PRIMARY AND SECONDARY REASONS FOR LEARNING THIS UNIQUE ART OF SELF-DEFENSE:

(1) just for self Defense & like to learn

(2)

OTHER

Curtis Arrayan
(NAME)

11/57
(DATE STARTED)

Oct 18 1938 — 18
(DATE OF BIRTH) (AGE)

Seronio Chief Instructor at Hilo, Sep 11, 1958

TO: MR. [illegible]

SUBJECT: TERMINATION OF INSTRUCTORSHIP UNDER
THE KAJUKENBO SELF-DEFENSE INSTITUTE

You are hereby informed of the release of your instructorship in Hilo, Hawaii under the Kajukenbo Self-Defense Institute Branch. As of this date, the class which you instructed is now owned and instructed by Mr. George Seronio thus terminating your instructorship and the use of the Kajukenbo Self-Defense Institute organizations' name.

It is now in the power of Mr. George Seronio to select his officials and assistant instructors, and to select a proper organization's name for the Hilo Kenpo-Karate Class.

I am requesting the return of the letter of the "Delegation of Authority" and your membership card of the Kajukenbo Self-Defense Institute.

Kindly submit it to Mr. George Seronio upon his arrival there in Hilo; which in turn upon his return to Honolulu, be forwarded to the Chief Instructor Mr. Adriano D. Emperado.

Lastly, I would like very much to commend you on your part in developing this unique art of self-defense and taking upon yourself the hardship and many hours of hard work to promote this art there in the island of Hawaii. You're doing a great job. Keep it up. Thank you, I remain

Dated: Honolulu, T.H. September 11, 1958

Fraternally yours,

Mr. Adriano D. Emperado
Black Belt Holder
Chief Instructor of the
Kajukenbo Self-Defense Institute

Mr. George Seronio
Owner of the Hilo Self-Defense
Organization

Mr. Alejo Reyes
Secretary-Treasury
Kajukenbo Self-Defense Institute

Distribution:
a. Mr. Adriano Emperado
b. Mr. George Seronio
c. Mr. Alejo Reyes

John Leoning Authority to Teach, May 1959

TO: WHOM IT MAY CONCERN

SUBJECT: DELEGATION OF AUTHORITY FOR
MR. JUAN (JOHN) LEONING

1. I hereby grant full authority to conduct Kenpo-Karate Classes in the United States of America.

2. Mr. Leoning accepts <u>all</u> responsibilities that may develop in his organization and that, I will <u>not</u> be responsible for any debts, taxes, and obligations incurred by him.

3. Any person under the teachings of Mr. Leoning <u>will agree</u> to waive any claims against the KAJUKENBO SELF-DEFENSE INSTITUTE <u>and</u> its representatives for any INJURIES and/or DEATH arising from or received during PRACTICE, REGULARLY SCHEDULED CLASSES or CONTEST.

4. It is now in the power of Mr. Leoning to select his officials and assistant instructors within his organization.

5. I have full Power of Attorney to foreclose this Delegation of Authority in event Mr. Leoning is unable to continue his instructorship of his organization due to unforseen circumstances.

Lastly, I would like very much to wish you all the luck and happiness. May you and your students, wherever you may be, train harder, and be greatly inspired by our almighty God in the teachings in the unique Art of the KENPO-KARATE DEFENSE.

Dated: Honolulu, Hawaii May 26, 1959

Fraternally Yours,

Mr. Adriano D. Emperado
Owner, Chief Instructor of the
Kajukenbo Self-Defense Institute
Emperado Kenpo-Karate Method

Distribution:
a. Mr. Adriano D. Emperado
b. Mr. Juan (John) Leoning
c. Mr. Aleju Reyes

Mr. Juan (John) Leoning
Representative
Kajukenbo Self-Defense Institute

Mr. Aleju Reyes
Witness
Secretary-Treasury
Kajukenbo Self-Defense Institute

Emperado's typed knife techniques

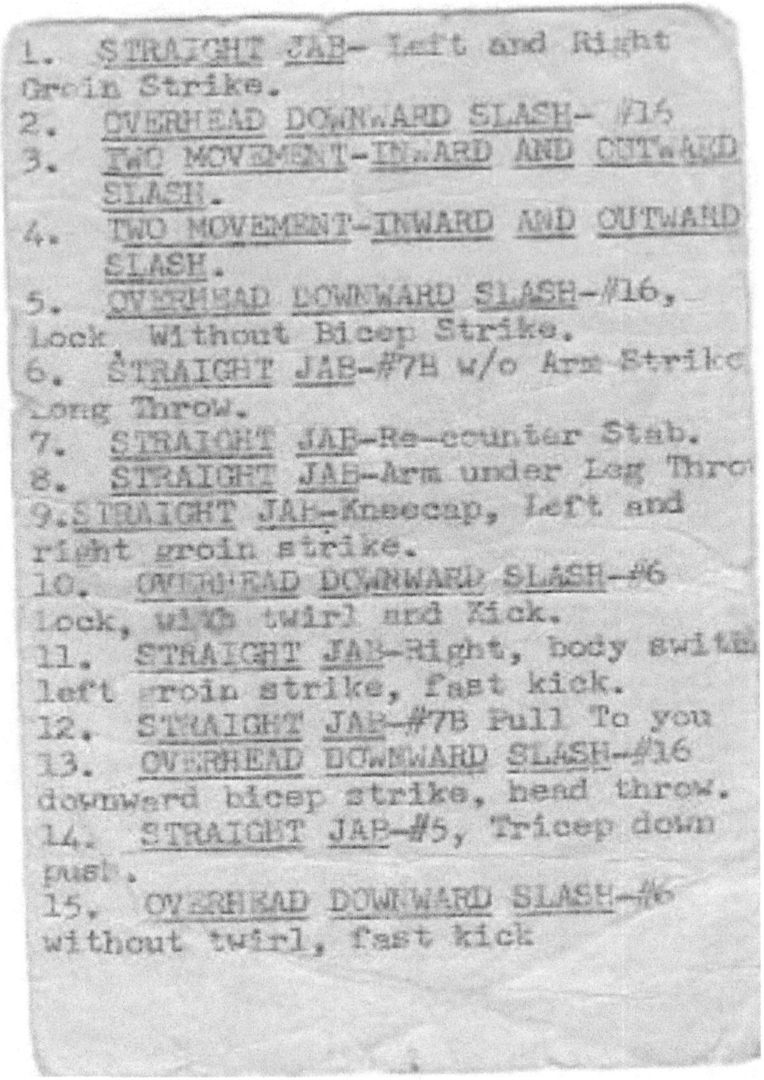

1. STRAIGHT JAB- Left and Right Groin Strike.
2. OVERHEAD DOWNWARD SLASH- #16
3. TWO MOVEMENT-INWARD AND OUTWARD SLASH.
4. TWO MOVEMENT-INWARD AND OUTWARD SLASH.
5. OVERHEAD DOWNWARD SLASH-#16, Lock, Without Bicep Strike.
6. STRAIGHT JAB-#7B w/o Arm Strike Long Throw.
7. STRAIGHT JAB-Re-counter Stab.
8. STRAIGHT JAB-Arm under Leg Throw
9. STRAIGHT JAB-Kneecap, Left and right groin strike.
10. OVERHEAD DOWNWARD SLASH-#6 Lock, with twirl and Kick.
11. STRAIGHT JAB-Right, body switch left groin strike, fast kick.
12. STRAIGHT JAB-#7B Pull To you
13. OVERHEAD DOWNWARD SLASH-#16 downward bicep strike, head throw.
14. STRAIGHT JAB-#5, Tricep down push.
15. OVERHEAD DOWNWARD SLASH-#6 without twirl, fast kick

Emperado handwritten club techniques

CLUB COUNTERS

1. TWO HAND CROSS - W/FAST RIGHT FOOT KICK.

2. TWO HAND CROSS - LEFT HAND TWIST, GRAB CLUB, POKE TO STOMACH. PLACE CLUB UNDER ARM TO THROAT FOR THROW.

3. #16, W/O GROIN STRIKE, HITTING THROAT HOLDING NECK AND ARM HIGH.

4. #16, GROIN STRIKE, ONE STEP RIGHT FOOT BACKWARDS FOR AN ARM BREAK SWING INTO A NECK CHOKE HOLDING NECK AND ARM HIGH.

[illegible] LEFT SIDE COVER, LEFT HAND OVER AND UNDER TO GRAB YOUR RIGHT HAND WRIST, [illegible] CLUB INTO SOLAR PLEXUS, PUSH UP [illegible]WARDS LEFT FOR A THROW TO FLOOR.

6. LEFT SIDE COVER, LEFT HAND GROIN STRIKE INTO LEFT HAND PUSH BACK OF HEAD SWINGING DOWNWARDS FOR A THROW ON HIS BACK.

A. LEFT SIDE COVER, #7A LONG THROW

RIGHT SIDE COVER, FAST WRIST STRIKE TO COLLAR BONE, GRAB HIS ARM AND DELIVER ELBOW SMASH TO HEAD FOR A THROW TO YOUR LEFT.

#16, GROIN STRIKE, ELBOW SMASH TO RIBS [illegible] TWIST W/FAST RIGHT KICK TO FACE, [illegible]ST STRIKE [illegible] TRICEP, SNAPPING [illegible] KNUCK[illegible] STRIKE TO BACK OF HE[illegible]

[illegible]

Emperado's KSDI 10th Degree, April 22, 1968

BE IT KNOWN TO ALL MEN:

That ADRIANO D. EMPERADO, originator of the Kajukenbo style of self-defense and founder of the Kajukenbo Self-Defense Institute, having met the moral, physical and spiritual standards of the Kajukenbo Self-Defense Institute, Inc., a non-profit organization organized and existing under and by virtue of the laws of the State of Hawaii, under the powers vested in us by the Creators of the Kajukenbo style of self-defense, and pursuant to the rules and regulations of the Kajukenbo Self-Defense Institute, Inc., because of his exemplification of the meaning of the teachings of Kajukenbo philosophy as represented by his SPIRIT, MIND and BODY, we, the BOARD OF DIRECTORS of Kajukenbo Self-Defense Institute, Inc., do hereby bestow upon ADRIANO D. EMPERADO the title of PROFESSOR and do further grant upon him the rank of TENTH DEGREE.

Be it further known that under the powers vested in this Board, we do hereby authorize and direct said PROFESSOR ADRIANO D. EMPERADO to teach the Kajukenbo style of Oriental Martial Arts to other worthy persons so that they too, like him, might promote the ideals and purposes of said organization for the good and betterment of all.

Robert T. Kawakami
Chairman
Frank Ordonez
Director
Benjamin Kekumu
Director

IN WITNESS WHEREOF, Robert T. Kawakami, Frank Ordonez and Benjamin Kekumu have respectively set their hands and the seal of theKajukenbo Self-Defense Institute, Inc., this 22nd day of April, 1968.

STATE OF HAWAII)
) ss
CITY AND COUNTY OF HONOLULU)

On this 22nd day of April, 1968, before me appeared Robert T. Kawakami, Frank Ordonez and Benjamin Kekumu to me personally known, who, being duly sworn by me, did say that they are the chairman of the Board and directors respectively of Kajukenbo Self-Defense Institute, Inc., and that the seal affixed to the foregoing instrument is the corporate seal and that said instrument was signed and sealed in behalf of said corporation by authority of its Board of Directors, and Robert Kawakami, Frank Ordonez and Benjamin Kekumu acknowledged said instrument to be the free act and deed of said corporation.

Notary Public, First Judicial Circuit, State of Hawaii.

INVESTIGATIVE RESOURCES

Adriano Emperado on USAT Goucher Victory, Oahu to Guadalcanal, Oct 31, 1947, Ancestry.com

Adriano Emperado on USAT General Pope, Guam to Honolulu, Jul 4, 1948, Ancestry.com

Adriano Emperado army discharge papers, National Personnel Records Center

"Beauty Queen-Violet Kutz." (1957, Dec 04). *Honolulu Star-Advertiser*, page 7.

Bishop, John. *Kajukenbo, The Original Mixed Martial Art*, InstantPublisher.com, 2006

Bishop, John. Emperado Speaks featuring Adriano Emperado and John Bishop, 1987: youtube.com/watch?v=G0Ul64sMGxM

"Choo's Daily Practice-Judo Lifts Veteran's Ring Hopes." (1953, Aug 12). *Stars and Stripes*

Frank Ordonez, army record, National Personnel Records Center

"Free Exhibition Thursday." (1952, Nov 11). *Honolulu Star-Bulletin*, page 20.

Founders interview featuring Adriano Emperado, Joseph Holck, Peter Choo, 1992: https://www.youtube.com/watch?v=8id27Ibanes

"Funeral Notice Emperado, Mr. Joseph Directo." (1958, Jun 03). *Honolulu Star-Advertiser*, page 16.

George Chang, army record, National Personnel Records Center

Haines, Bruce. *Karate and its Development in Hawaii to 1959*, a thesis at the University of Hawaii, 1962

"Hawaiian Uses Head on Bricks." (1959, May 30). *Daily Kenrim*

"Hawaii GIs In Service." (1947, Aug 28). *Honolulu Star-Bulletin*, page 14.

Joseph Holck, army service record, National Personnel Records Center

"Joseph Holck Image"
www.danzan.com/HTML/People/Kufferath.html
"Judo Championships of N. California Here Tomorrow." (1950, Mar 18). *Stockton Evening and Sunday Record,* page 11.
Kajukenbo Founders Interview
https://www.bing.com/videos/riverview/relatedvideo?&q=John+Bishop+kajukenbo&&mid=BEF4312250ADCE21F431BEF4312250ADCE21F431&&FORM=VRDGA
"Kenpo Club Seeks Queen Contestants for Benefit Dance." (1957, Nov 27). *Honolulu Star-Bulletin*, page 13.
"Learn Judo." (1955, Jan 22). *Hattiesburg American*, page 11.
"Legal Notices, In the office of the Governor of the Territory of Hawaii-Decree." (1943, Feb 11).*Honolulu Star Bulletin*, page 11.
Mitose, James M., *What is Self-Defense? (Kenpo Jiu-Jitsu)*, Kosho-Shorei Publishing Company, 1981
Ordonez Kajukenbo Ohana website:
https://www.ordonezkajukenbo.org/
Panther Productions interview featuring Emperado, Gary Forbach, and Joseph Jennings,
ENTREVISTA DE 1987 A SIJO ADRIANO EMPERADO FUNDADOR DEL KAJUKENBO
Peter Choo army service record, National Personnel Records Center
"Self-Defense Group Elects Officials." (1957, Dec 28). *Honolulu Star-Advertiser*, page 9.
Tavares, David. *Black Robe, The Kempo/Kajukenbo Connection*, www.Black-Robe.net, 2017
The Sijo Emperado Interview for Centuron Negro by John Bishop. (Retrieved on 2025, Feb 08).
http://www.cqbkajukenbo, The Sijo-emperado-interview-from/
"Waikakalaua Fites Tonight." (1944, Feb 11). *Honolulu Advertiser*
"108-Funeral Notices, Kawakami, Robert Tadashi, Twinkle." (1996, Dec 04). *Honolulu Star-Advertiser,* page 30.

CONTRIBUTORS

Glen Fraticelli, Deputy Chief of the Kajukenbo Self-Defense Institute, photos and documents:

- Foreword photo
- Adriano Emperado, Peter Choo, and George Chang photos
- Wahiawa school photo
- Frank Ordonez and Mas Oyama photo
- Woodrow McCandless, Benny Madiros, and Adriano Emperado photo
- George Seronio certificate for the Hilo school
- John Leoning authority to teach certificate
- Adriano Emperado unpublished book excerpt
- Adriano Emperado typed and written technique documents

Albert Saddler (Seronio family) photos and documents:

- Palama Settlement photo
- Adriano Emperado, Joe Emperado, Woodrow McCandless, and George Seronio photos
- Wahiawa school admission forms
- George Seronio black belt book photos

Other Contributors:

- Al Dacascos photo approval courtesy of Al Dacascos

- Joe Emperado and Marino Tiwanak photos courtesy of John Lianos
- Tony Ramos photos courtesy of David Amiccuci and Leah Ramos Amiccuci
- Joe Emperado funeral photo courtesy of David Amiccuci and Leah Ramos Amiccuci
- Charles Gaylord photos courtesy of Kelly Gaylord McCormick
- John Leoning photo courtesy of Carlos Bunda
- Joe Halbuna photo courtesy of Ilona Halbuna
- Aleju Reyes photo courtesy of Joseph Davis
- John Kanehailua and John Pascua photos courtesy of John Kanehailua

"As long as Kajukenbo is still alive in this country and the world, I am still alive."

Adriano Emperado

PALAMA SETTLEMENT

Joe Emperado   Adriano Emperado

Made in the USA
Coppell, TX
22 January 2026